The FIFTIES *and* SIXTIES

The *FIFTIES* and SIXTIES

a lifestyle revolution

Miriam Akhtar and Steve Humphries

BXTREE

To all those who lent us their memories. Thank you.

ACKNOWLEDGEMENTS

We would like to thank all the people who have helped with the book and the television series it accompanies. Special thanks to David Liddiment, ITV Director of Programmes and Dianne Nelmes, Controller of Documentaries and Features at ITV, for making it all possible. Thanks also to Jane Devane and Georgia Love at ITV and Natasha Roe at LWT for their help.

We are grateful for the hard work, goodwill, the talent and the imagination of everyone who has worked on this project at Testimony Films. Thanks to inspirational editor Daniel de Waal and to the excellent research team of Nick Maddocks, Gill Hennessey, Maree Came, Ellen Quinn, Roz Sinclair, Cassie Belham, Lisa Hanel, Jenny Mitchell and Katie Harns. Thanks also to Madge Reed for transcriptions, Mike Humphries for production management, Mike Pharey who filmed most of the interviewees and to Steve Haskett who filmed some of them, together with sound provided by Alexis Cardes and Tony Brown. And thanks to Stephen and Olive Peet and to Linda Shanovitch for providing locations.

For general advice and assistance we would like to thank Marguerite Patten, David Harrison and Tim Davey of the *Bristol Evening Post*, Chris Williams, Robert Opie, Monique Lentier, Lesley Gillilan, James Smith, Philip Vaughan, Miriam Walsh, Gill Sheppard, Alison Mercer, Paul Pierrot, Miranda Steed, Shona Harris, John Ruthven, Jan Faull and the staff of the BFI National Film and Television Archive, Stephen Vokins of the National Motor Museum and Rob Perks of the National Life Stories Collection. Finally thanks to Emma Marriott, senior editor at Boxtree for her support and work on the book.

PICTURE CREDITS

The publishers would like to thank the following agencies for permission to reproduce their images:

The Advertising Archive Limited - pages 32, 39, 52, 54, 59, 64, 66, 76, 92, 98, 117, 126, 147, 181; Corbis Images – pages 2, 3, 36, 42, 44, 53, 105, 153, 154, 160; Hulton Archive – pages 15, 37, 40, 51, 60, 62, 67, 69, 91, 94, 97, 111, 115, 130, 131, 151, 157, 162, 163, 168, 174, 179, 187; National Motor Museum, Beaulieu – pages 159, 165; Popperfoto – pages 12, 17, 24, 27, 35, 57, 75, 79, 81, 82, 83, 100, 103, 123, 144, 148, 166, 171, 172; Robert Opie – pages 18, 21, 23, 28, 31, 45, 80, 85, 87, 89, 90, 104 , 106, 108, 109, 112, 118, 119, 132, 134, 137, 139, 141, 143, 144, 152, 158, 177; Topham Picturepoint – pages 14, 47, 48, 71, 96, 114, 122, 124 , 128.

First published 2001 by Boxtree,
an imprint of Pan Macmillan Ltd

Pan Macmillan
20 New Wharf Road
London N1 9RR

Basingstoke and Oxford

Associated companies throughout the world

www.panmacmillan.com

ISBN 0 7522 6191 6

Text © Miriam Akhtar & Steve Humphries

9 8 7 6 5 4 3 2 1

A CIP catalogue record for this book is available from the British Library.

Design by Isobel Gillan

Colour reproduction by Aylesbury Studios

Printed in Great Britain by Butler and Tanner Ltd, Frome and London

The book accompanies the television series
The Fifties and Sixties made by Testimony Films for ITV.

Producers – Steve Humphries and Miriam Akhtar

Contents

Introduction

I T WAS 2 JUNE 1953. THIS WAS THE FIRST DAY OF THE NEW Elizabethan age. The 25-year-old princess was crowned Queen Elizabeth II amidst scenes of national celebration, the like of which had not been seen since VE Day. The Coronation seemed to symbolise renewed hope for the future and a spirit of national unity that had helped Britain win the war. Many believed that their country might achieve unprecedented greatness and new prosperity under the young Queen. This was the first great television event in twentieth-century Britain. More than twenty million watched the ceremony on their black-and-white televisions, many of which had been bought specially for the occasion. This was followed by street parties in towns and villages the length and breadth of the land. Bunting and Union Jacks were hanging from almost every window and street lamp, and every child had been given a Coronation mug.

Schoolgirls wore red, white and blue ribbons. In the evening bonfires were lit on prominent hills, including Ben Nevis, forming a blazing chain of beacons all over Britain. It seemed to signal a bright future for a nation that was now trying to forget the privations of war and rationing. In fact what left the most indelible mark on the children was not the royal pomp but the trestle tables, laden with luxury food for them to feast on. Looking back the street party fare seems modest in the extreme. But to boys and girls brought up on ration books and food shortages, it was positively decadent.

'I'll always remember the Coronation because Coronation Day in 1953 was my seventh birthday,' says Frank Perry from Manchester. 'We had a new television to watch it on, it was only a tiny thing with a nine-inch screen and a flickering picture, but we thought it was wonderful. All our neighbours came in to watch because we had the only television in the block of flats where we lived. We had rows of chairs lined up in our living room packed out with people. Then we had a street party, the mums set up trestle tables with meat pies, there was sausage rolls and fairy cakes. What was so great though, there were sweets as well. Somebody brought a complete jar of sweets and because they were still rationed that was a rare treat. We kids got one apiece. And I had my first ever pear drop. I loved it.'

The Coronation was on the cusp of a major change in modern British history. The fifties and sixties were watershed years. Britain changed from a land that was war-torn, bleak and economically depressed into one that was more affluent, confident and colourful. The change in photography during these years from black-and-white to colour almost acts as a metaphor for the period. By the late sixties most people were taking colour photographs and colour cine cameras were all the rage. BBC 2 began transmitting in colour in 1967 followed by BBC 1 and ITV in 1969. Everything seemed more colourful whether it was clothes, cars or home décor. There was a real spirit of change, a sense of adventure and excitement. Many of the conventions of the past were swept away. Britain shed its old identity as a deeply conservative nation and adopted a new one as international fashion leader. It became a trailblazer for youth, hedonism and modernity.

Of course not all the youthful optimism was justified. Some of the new ideas created more problems than they solved. A few, like the sixties obsession with razing inner-city working class communities to the ground and replacing them with tower block estates, were positively disastrous. The new aspiration towards a more home-centred lifestyle led to a weakening of old communal ties and customs. But overall there was a huge improvement in our way of life. Much of it was financed by the economic boom of the never-had-it-so-good years. There was full employment and wages were rising rapidly for almost everyone. This was the period when the benefits of the welfare state and the National Health Service, first established in 1948, kicked in too. By the end of the sixties most people were better housed, better fed and healthier than in the past. Much of the drudgery and hardship of everyday life was removed by a new sophisticated network of electricity throughout the country and mod cons in the home. There was greater mobility and independence with the arrival of mass car-ownership. Britain had become a more liberal place to live. The majority enjoyed more freedom and more choices than ever before, and it resulted in a revolution in our lifestyle.

In this book and the television series it accompanies we try to provide a fresh overview of the fifties and sixties by making extensive use of personal testimony. Through our research we have collected stories from over two thousand men and women. This makes it one of the most comprehensive oral histories of the period. Most of those we quote initially wrote to us in answer to our call for memories of the fifties and sixties published in national and local newspapers all over Britain. The most quoted voices are usually those that we filmed and who appeared in the television series. They were chosen because of the vividness of their memories and the power of their stories. We believe that they represent a broad spectrum of the nation's experience during these two momentous decades. We have generally excluded the rich and the famous and the much-quoted sixties icons – this is a social history of the unseen and unheard majority. We hear from the ordinary boys and girls who grew up then, from the early teenage rebels, from the first-time home-owners and car-drivers, from the pioneering DIY enthusiasts and from the first generation of girls to go on the Pill. We have also tried to steer away from the overwhelming focus on London – especially sixties 'Swinging London' – which dominates many histories of the period. Instead, we have tried to tell the story of Britain as a whole and have drawn on accounts from all over the country. Similarly we have not just concentrated on young people. The fifties and sixties were very different according to how old you were as well as what part of the country you lived in. We have tried to reflect this diversity of experience across all ages, areas and classes.

Each chapter explores a key theme in British life during the fifties and sixties. We begin with the more child-centred world that emerged in the post-war years, lovingly remembered by many as a golden age of innocence and simple pleasures. Although some of the old disciplinarian attitudes continued, this really was a time when children were better cared for and protected than ever before. It is no coincidence that the baby boomers, who had been brought up in a more liberal and caring atsmosphere, became the freedom loving teenagers of the sixties. The driving force behind the new teen scene was the money and the time that young people now had to spare. They used it to develop their own music, their own fashions and their own lifestyle. The world of the teenager in the late sixties was unrecognizable to that of their counterparts in the early fifties, when young people dressed like their parents and, on the whole, did as their parents told them.

The bedrock for many of the improvements in the British way of life came with the housing revolution prompted by the post-war housing crisis and the lack of suitable public homes. Twenty years of sustained public building followed and much of it, on new council estates and in new towns, provided a much higher standard of comfort and convenience than the overcrowded, bug-infested working-class homes of the past. However in the fifties and sixties a new dream was emerging – home-ownership. Members of the more affluent younger generation aspired to a home of their own and this began to shape the modern ideal of married life. In 1950 there were just over three million home-owners, but by the late sixties this had mushroomed to over eight million. This was a time when home life was revolutionized by the arrival of mains electricity and mod cons which reduced the daily drudgery of washing, cleaning and cooking for the housewife.

Now she was expected to be a kitchen queen using her gas or electric oven to conjure up more sophisticated, continental-style dishes for her husband and family. After the long years of rationing, food and drink were the glittering prizes of the new consumer society. Many fifties housewives aspired to be domestic goddesses, but by the sixties the dream of culinary perfection was beginning to fade. Women were feeling trapped and many preferred to return to work. Their liberation from the home was aided by the rise of convenience foods and supermarkets. Fast foods and drinks became all the rage which was all very exciting, but it wasn't very healthy. And for some there was a price to pay as the nation embarked on a mass binge of fatty, sugary convenience foods.

Much of the increased earning power of couples was spent on the home. The fifties and sixties were a time when home design and furnishing became a popular obsession, especially for the new breed of homeowners. Most favoured the modern, contemporary look. Walls came down, rooms were opened up, fireplaces were ripped out, picture rails and skirting boards disappeared. The new cult of DIY was established, taking advantage of the plastics revolution. Formica became the buzzword of the age. The period detail of Victorian and Edwardian homes vanished under a sea of hardboard. But by the mid-sixties a reaction had set in and fashionable middle-class couples were busy restoring Victorian cottages and suburban homes to their former glory.

The British were now spending more and more time at home. This was the period when watching the television became firmly established as the nation's favourite way to spend its free time. In the early fifties there was only one television station, the BBC, and only 350,000 households had television sets. This was the heyday of the cinema and Hollywood epics, and spectator sports also drew huge crowds. The wireless was the most popular form of home entertainment. The fifties and sixties saw a battle between the Bakelite, the big screen and the box for the hearts and minds of the British people. By the late sixties television had won hands down – practically the entire population owned a television and watched it most evenings.

This was also an era when people wanted to get away from home and travel when they liked. Having their own set of wheels was a passport to this freedom and car-ownership increased ten times in just twenty years. The British fell in love with the car – and out of love with public transport. The car, once restricted to the wealthy, came within the reach of the majority of families, and women drove in greater numbers. However, the car-owning society brought new problems of traffic congestion and a terrible increase in road accidents. By the late sixties new restrictions on drink-driving and compulsory seat belts helped to reduce the carnage. The roads remained dangerous but there was no going back. Britain had become a nation of car owners and most people relished the greater independence and mobility they now enjoyed.

The most sensational lifestyle change of the sixties was the sexual revolution: what had once been a private act became a public obsession. Sex became the ultimate personal pleasure and increasing numbers demanded the right to sexual fulfilment inside and outside marriage. With the coming of the Pill there was a blossoming of sexual freedom and experimentation amongst young people, and we draw on the experiences of our interviewees to tell the story of how sexual attitudes in Britain were transformed during the fifties and sixties. There was a big increase in the sexual expectations of both men and women. Many were not prepared to put up with the sexual privations of the past. Sexual choice had become part of the modern lifestyle.

chapter

The **Baby Boomers**

THE FIFTIES AND SIXTIES WERE THE YEARS OF THE baby boomers, the children of the post-war bulge in the birth rate. Many of them – and their parents – now lovingly remember particularly the fifties as a golden age of childhood. Nothing epitomizes this more than cherished memories of a natural, innocent and safe world of play. 'We'd go down to the park every afternoon on our bikes,' recalls May Hedges from Cheshire. 'We'd take sandwiches and home-made lemonade and go fishing for tiddlers in the brook.' There were few toys compared to today, but there were many games to be played in the streets and the fields; trees to be climbed, streams to be dammed and woods to hide in. 'The children would go off into the fields for hours,' says Margaret Birkin from Stroud, 'and then when it was time to eat, I'd send the dog out with a note attached to his collar – "come home, dinner is ready".'

Previous page The fifties roller skate craze. This was the decade when modern childhood really began to take shape.

There were also the bucket-and-spade joys of the family seaside holiday. The annual pilgrimage of mum, dad and the children to British seaside resorts enjoyed a final heyday during this decade and most families returned to the same resort or holiday camp year after year. Blackpool, which received seven million holidaymakers a year, was the Mecca for Lancashire's mill towns. Wherever they went, most people recall long, sunny days when it never seemed to rain. After the deprivations of war and rationing, the simple pleasures of the sun, sea and sand tasted that much sweeter. Some aspects of childhood in those days have undoubtedly been mythologized. Nevertheless, most children had never had it so good – the fifties was the decade when modern childhood really began to take shape.

A LABOUR *of Love*

Mother and baby pose in the early fifties. Mothers were encouraged to lavish love on their newborn.

From the moment they were born the baby-boom children of the 1950s and 1960s grew up in a more child-centred world than ever before. Victorian attitudes that children should be 'seen and not heard' were still around, but they were losing their influence. The old regimented methods of feeding and toilet-training by the clock were on the way out and were being replaced by a softer, more liberal and natural approach. Fifties mothers were encouraged to pick babies up when they cried. Infants were allowed to explore their environment and express themselves through creative play. Benjamin Spock's *The Common Sense Book of Baby and Child Care*, first published in 1946, was a bestseller amongst the new breed of British parents. It struck just the right note after the war, when children were seen as especially precious. Parents were determined to give them a better life than they had enjoyed, and although there was still strict discipline and physical punishment in many homes, this came to be seen as a last

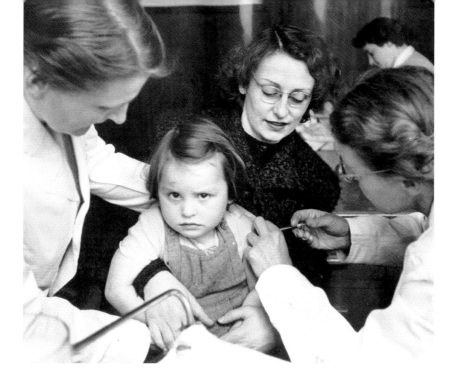

A reluctant looking girl is given a polio vaccination in 1956 – a year when there was a massive vaccination programme to stave off the polio epidemic.

resort. Most important was an atmosphere of tender loving care. One mothercraft specialist writing in the April 1952 edition of *Housewife* magazine advised that, 'firmness is one of the least useful attitudes of a good parent and certainly not nearly so important as sympathy, understanding, patience and skill'. This was very different from the advice given to previous generations of parents. It was the way of the future.

Welfare STATE

Fifties children also benefited hugely from the new welfare state. The National Health Service, introduced in 1948, provided free medical care for women and children for the first time. This, combined with advances in medicine, extensive immunization programmes and improvements in housing and hygiene, led to a steady decline in infant deaths. The number of young lives lost through traditional killer diseases also reduced rapidly – whooping cough, diphtheria, scarlet fever and measles were all on the wane. Poor working-class children benefited the most. Regular medical inspections at school, dental check-ups and eye examinations meant that the fifties child enjoyed much better health than a boy or girl born at the beginning of the century.

The only dark cloud on the horizon was the polio epidemic of the fifties, which claimed the lives of 2500 children and disabled several thousand more before a cure was found. But with the welfare state now providing medical care, everything was done to help the young victims. 'I think I caught it from playing near the sewage pipes on Seaburn beach,' says Josephine Dingwall

> ONE DAY AFTER WE'D BEEN TO THE BEACH I FELT VERY POORLY. I COULDN'T WALK. TO BEGIN WITH THEY THOUGHT IT WAS RHEUMATISM BUT THEN IT WAS DIAGNOSED AS POLIO. I WAS PARALYSED FROM THE WAIST DOWN. I COULDN'T WALK AT ALL, WHICH WAS TERRIBLE FOR A SMALL CHILD. I WENT TO NEWCASTLE ROAD HOSPITAL IN SUNDERLAND EVERYDAY AFTER SCHOOL AND THEY GAVE ME PHYSIOTHERAPY.

from Sunderland. 'We always went there with the family on Saturdays in summer and one day after we'd been to the beach I felt very poorly. I couldn't walk. To begin with they thought it was rheumatism but then it was diagnosed as polio. I was paralysed from the waist down. I couldn't walk at all, which was terrible for a small child. I went to Newcastle Road Hospital in Sunderland everyday after school and they gave me physiotherapy. They did lots of exercises to flex my muscles and make my legs more supple. They put me in a dome filled with light bulbs to warm me. They thought that was a great help, whether it was or not I don't know. And I had operations on my feet. The only frightening thing was the matron. She was so strict. If I had to stay overnight in the hospital for treatment I was terrified of her. She'd come round the ward at night with a torch and you felt your heart beating fast. You didn't dare open your eyes even though you weren't asleep. The nurses and doctors, though ... they were all so caring and lovely to me. They did everything they could to help me and it was because of what they did that I started to walk again.'

Bringing Up BABY

Fifties children probably received more individual care and attention from their mothers than those of any previous generation. With the average couple restricting themselves to two or three children – far fewer than earlier in the century – there was more time to spend on each one. This was also the decade of the full-time housewife and mother. Only one in five married women went out to work in 1951. Some who had endured years of exhausting war work were relieved to be staying at home. Others had no choice as many employers adopted a 'jobs for the boys' policy. In any case, fifties thinking about child-rearing encouraged mothers to believe it was their duty to be at home for their children. Dr John Bowlby's *Child Care and the Growth of Love*, published in 1953, was hugely influential. In it he contended that constant mother love was a vital factor in the formation of a child's character and that if it was absent juvenile delinquency was the likely result. This message was backed up by all the women's magazines of the time. Many married women came to feel oppressed by this domestic bondage, especially as their children grew older, and by the late 1950s one

The fifties were the era of the full-time housewife and mother.

in three had returned to work. But their presence in the home undoubtedly led to closer relationships with their children. Mum was, quite literally, always there for them.

'I really looked forward to going home to my mum,' remembers John Gardner from South Gloucestershire. 'She would let me come home every lunchtime from school. I could always choose what I wanted. Sometimes it was just boiled egg and bread soldiers, but it was a lovely break from school. If I felt really ill I knew I could stay at home in the afternoon because Mum would be there to look after me. And when me and my brother came home from school Mum would sometimes take us out for walks. When I was eight she got a part-time job and I couldn't come home any more. It was school dinners from then on and I really missed her. We had to go to Nan's house after school and she was much stricter. That wasn't half so much fun.'

> "
>
> I REALLY LOOKED FORWARD TO GOING HOME TO MY MUM. SHE WOULD LET ME COME HOME EVERY LUNCHTIME FROM SCHOOL. I COULD ALWAYS CHOOSE WHAT I WANTED. SOMETIMES IT WAS JUST BOILED EGG AND BREAD SOLDIERS, BUT IT WAS A LOVELY BREAK FROM SCHOOL. IF I FELT REALLY ILL I KNEW I COULD STAY AT HOME IN THE AFTERNOON BECAUSE MUM WOULD BE THERE TO LOOK AFTER ME.
>
> "

There was more time for play, too, for the fifties child. Until then most children had jobs to do when they weren't at school. Boys generally worked for cash – they took newspaper rounds, ran errands, helped with deliveries and were hired as seasonal labour in the countryside. Poorer working-class boys often had several jobs on the go at the same time and their earnings could be vital in the family's struggle for survival. Girls' jobs were equally important, but were generally unpaid. This was because they were done around the home – daughters helped with wash days and with cooking and cleaning, and played little mother to younger brothers and sisters. However, from the fifties onwards greater affluence and the spread of labour-saving devices reduced the need for children to work. They were less likely to earn money themselves and were given it by their parents. Pocket money came to be seen as their right. 'It started when I was seven and went up every year on my birthday,' says Peter Dixon from Newcastle. 'It wasn't much, but it was enough to buy sweets and comics and go to football matches. Mum and Dad thought I should perhaps give them a bit of help doing some chores for it. I always found an excuse to get out of it though. I always wanted to go out playing football and cricket. I was such a disaster around the home anyway, I was always dropping plates and breaking things and bumping into people, eventually they gave up and didn't ask any more. So it was money for nothing.'

What's in the TOYBOX?

Children also came to expect presents on birthdays, and even more at Christmas. Before the war their birthdays had been little celebrated in working-class families, who couldn't afford the expense. And even at Christmas most toys they were given were home-made or hand-me-downs. But in the never-had-it-so-good years of the fifties all this was to change and many parents indulged their children as never before. Lavish present-giving was all part of the new celebration of childhood.

The result was a boom in businesses producing goods for the modern child-consumer. After the privations of rationing and austerity they brought much-needed

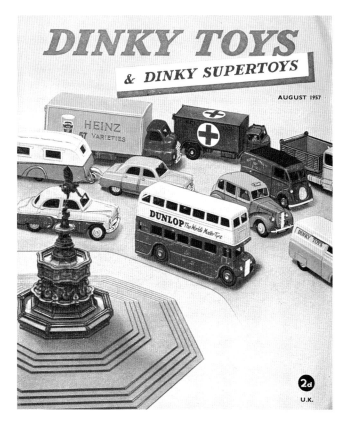

colour and choice into children's lives. Many firms were set up soon after the war. One of the most successful was Lesney Products, formed by ex-Royal Navy sailors Leslie Smith and Rodney Smith together with former army engineer Jack Odell. Their breakthrough came in 1953 when they made a million scale models of the Queen's Coronation coach. They followed up with the fantastically successful Matchbox series of models aimed at boys. There was a fairly rigid gender demarcation and most toys were produced for either boys or girls. Other favourites, also for boys, were Dinky toys, the most popular die-cast model vehicles of the fifties. Corgi toys, which began in 1956, achieved huge sales through their close attention to detail in their model cars. Glue-together Airfix kits were launched in 1952 and some of their bestsellers were models of RAF aircraft that had helped to win the war. Another fifties favourite was Subbuteo table soccer. One of the most expensive presents for boys was the Hornby Dublo train set. Before the war model railways had been largely restricted to well-to-do middle-class families. Now parents from all walks of life were buying them for their sons. 'I got a Hornby Dublo train set for my Christmas present when I was nine,' says Paul Parker from Stoke-on-Trent. 'Dad nailed the track down to a piece of hardboard in my bedroom and that stayed there for the next five years. Every birthday and Christmas I'd make an elaborate list of what I wanted –

A cavalcade of Dinky toys. In the fifties they were one of the most popular toys for boys, found in almost every home – now they are collectors' items.

an engine, a carriage, a signal, a station – all with the exact prices by the side, it was all carefully researched. I spent most of my young schooldays dreaming about my train set, making up timetables, pretending I was driving this little train, it seemed so exciting at the time. And there was real competition amongst boys as to how big your train set was and what engines you had. I didn't have as big a set as some of my classmates so I lied to keep up with them. The problem was I couldn't invite them back to our house and have them up to my room because they'd realise then that I'd been lying.'

Boys' toys encouraged action and adventure – to be an engine-driver was still the dream of many fifties schoolboys. Most girls' toys, however, reflected the caring, domestic role that was a woman's lot in those days. It was pure Janet and John. Amongst the most popular toys for girls were, predictably, dolls and their accessories. The widespread use of plastics meant they became ever more sophisticated with hair, blinking eyes and a range of outfits. When the Hula-Hoop craze swept Britain in 1958, toy manufacturers made a fortune from Hula dolls like the clockwork Spin-a-Hoop. Dolls' houses, cookery sets and nurses' uniforms were also bestsellers.

Who Wants to COME OUT TO PLAY?

These children's toys encouraged more home-based play and childhood games were becoming much more commercialized. Before the 1950s most boys and girls had spent much of their time playing outdoors with their friends. Street football and cricket, hopscotch, skipping, fighting, marbles, conkers, cowboys and Indians and a hundred other games had been the staples that occupied children's free time. This tradition carried on, but was less widespread than before. Now it was found only in poorer working-class areas with overcrowded homes and few toys, where the children's social lives and entertainments revolved around the street. Tommy Smith grew up in the Glasgow Gorbals in the fifties. 'To be kept in, not to be allowed out on the streets to play, that was a real deterrent. If it was a nice sunny day you'd look out of the window and see all your friends laughing and having fun and you're sitting there with nothing to do. We loved it in the streets. There were street gangs and each had their own territory, but you'd always try and sneak on to their patch and pinch something. Then they'd try and ambush you and chase you out. Sometimes you got a slap. You had to be tough, you had to hit back, otherwise there was no respect for you and your life would be hell. I got a lot of respect because I was quite a good artist from when I was very young. I'd do drawings on the pavement and on the walls. They'd say, "Tommy, do a drawing of Popeye, do Desperate Dan, do Cowboys and Indians," that sort of thing. And sometimes they'd give me sweets for it. To not go out and enjoy all that was terrible. I remember a lot of times sitting in the house in front of the coal fire and I'd get old broken soldiers and put them on the fire and watch them melt for something to do. My mum used to go off her head.'

By the late fifties, more and more play was indoors and revolving around the family. A number of social developments promoted this trend. Homes were becoming more comfortable and family size was reducing, so there was more space to play at home. At the same time, the rapid increase in motor traffic was restricting the space outside and making street play more difficult and dangerous. With electric light in the home, more comfortable chairs and more money to spend on books, fifties children spent more time reading at home. One supremely popular author of the fifties was Enid Blyton. These were the days when Noddy, the Famous Five and the Secret Seven captured the imagination of millions of young children. They were innocent, wholesome adventures and the well-mannered heroes embodied the ethos of the day. Most fifties books aimed at moral education and improvement, and celebrated public-school values of fair play, gentlemanly conduct and patriotism.

The *Eagle*, launched in 1950, featured the adventures of Dan Dare, who every week battled it out with his companion Digby against evil extraterrestrials.

Comic CRAZE

This was also true of the new children's comics. One of the most popular was the *Eagle*, launched in April 1950 and priced 3d. It was the creation of the Reverend Marcus Morris, who wanted to provide boys with a morally uplifting alternative to the glut of American comics that had taken hold in Britain just after the war. On the cover each week were the adventures of the space

traveller Dan Dare. With his companion Digby he battled it out against evil extraterrestrials. Other new comics for boys were *Swift*, *Lion* and *Tiger*. The star of *Tiger* was Roy of the Rovers. His trademark was scoring goals from impossible angles in the dying seconds of matches and he was part of the fantasy life of many a fifties boy. For girls there was *Girl*, *Girl's Crystal* and *School Friend*. *Bunty* joined these in 1958, offering a free ladybird ring with its opening issue. It was all pretty tame stuff by modern standards. Even comics like the *Beano*, whose characters were amongst the most anarchic and rebellious on offer, were ultimately humbled by authority figures. The final frames of Dennis the Menace and the Bash Street Kids inevitably showed the boys outwitted and punished by their adult enemies.

It is difficult to see fifties comics as being in any way subversive. But some parents and teachers did, and stopped children from reading them. 'I wasn't allowed comics,' remembers Londoner Linda Shanovitch. 'My parents saw them as a sort of dumbing down. They felt I should be reading a real book, not looking at pictures. I remember that I saved up the money that I got for my birthday and bought the *Bunty* annual. But as soon as my parents saw it they made me take it back to the shop.' The *Eagle* was banned by the grammar school near Graham Bill's home in Staffordshire. 'The boarders couldn't get hold of it because the local shops close to the school had been instructed not to stock them or serve them. So I used to buy copies of the *Eagle*, then I'd meet the boarders in the Spinney, which was a wooded bank alongside the canal. And I used to sell it to them or charge them for a read. That's how I made some extra money.'

HOBBYMANIA

Fifties boys and girls were encouraged to fill their free time with hobbies. Ideally – from the parents' point of view – these should be educational and improving. Stamp collecting became more popular than ever before. So, too, did Meccano. Although most hobbies were home-based, some – and the books that encouraged them – took children out of doors to explore the world around them. One involved the *I-Spy* books, the brainchild of retired headmaster Charles Warrell, the self-styled Big Chief I-Spy. Through his books children pretended to be Indian braves whose tasks were to spot different varieties of birds, animals, trees, aircraft, cars, buses, roads and signposts. By the late fifties the I-Spy tribe numbered half a million.

Meccano, one of the favourite home-based hobbies for boys in the fifties.

MECCANO

The Toy that grows with the Boy

U.K. 1957

23

the baby boomers

As a ten-year-old Dorothy Robson was a keen car spotter in the village of Oswaldtwistle in Lancashire. 'The main problem was that there weren't many cars to spot. You'd wait for them coming through and you'd think "Oh here's old Tom Broughton's car again" and we knew his number plate off by heart. It was the same with all the locals. But then if a stranger's car came through the village, that was so unusual. We'd think, just imagine if there's been a robbery down at the bank, and we'd take the number and a description down. Perhaps two men, one wearing a black jacket, and we'd note down how fast the car was going. It never came to anything but it gave us a wonderful time.'

Equally popular was trainspotting. In the last days of steam it was all the rage amongst boys – there were very few girl trainspotters and even at the time they viewed this curious male hobby with incredulity and condescension. The ultimate aim was to collect the number of every train. It involved young boys – sometimes accompanied by fathers or teachers – travelling to many faraway stations in search of new train numbers. This provided children with a mobility and a source of adventure that would have been out of the question for most of them before the war. Pocket money was avidly saved. And some trainspotters travelled as far as 300 miles a week. Ian Allen's Locospotters' Club reached 82,000 members in 1952 and the *ABC Locomotives* books topped 50,000 copies in 1954. But some boys became so obsessed they were prepared to sacrifice life and limb to get numbers. After two deaths at Nottingham station when children fell on the tracks, railway officials banned trainspotters from Crewe, then the busiest and most popular station for devotees. At Clapham Junction, another popular haunt, trainspotters were penned into a wire cage at the end of a platform. On some occasions there were actually arrests: in 1952 seven spotters were fined two shillings and sixpence (twelve pence) each at Derby for trespassing.

SWEET *Temptation*

Whilst children were following their favourite hobbies they were invariably eating sweets – consumption had soared with the end of sugar and chocolate rationing in the early fifties. The old pre-war favourites like toffees and sherbert fountains remained popular but, with new television advertising campaigns aimed at the child consumer, branded and heavily marketed sweets and chocolate bars came to dominate. Each had a catchphrase to promote it. Amongst the favourites were Mars ('a Mars a day helps you work rest and play') and Milky Way ('the sweet you can eat between meals'). Phrases like

these were tailor-made for children to use as ammunition to break down their parents' resistance to buying chocolate for them. Helen Parry from Colchester remembers: 'The main reason Mum gave for not buying chocolate was that it would spoil your appetite and you wouldn't eat all your dinner up. "Well, a Milky Way won't hurt then, will it, Mum?" It was the same with Mars bars. Mum said chocolate was bad for me, but eating Mars bars was going to make me do well at everything like Mum wanted. It all gave you a lot more pester power.'

Short Trousers, LONG SOCKS

One of the defining features of fifties children was their asexuality. Their clothes were designed to distinguish them from adults, and hence from the sexuality attached to the world of adults. Most boys wore short trousers. These had come into vogue in the 1920s and 1930s, partly as a result of the growing popularity of the Boy Scouts and school sports. The day-to-day clothes of girls were chosen to be practical rather than attractive, and dresses tended to be loose, unadorned and unstylish. Many people look back nostalgically to this era as a time when children could still be children. There was a simple innocence to childhood. Boys and girls could play childish games without worrying about how attractive they looked. Or whether anyone fancied them. These children, scrubbed and eager, often yearned for adventure – and found at least some in the ranks of the uniformed youth movements. In the fifties the Cubs, Brownies, Boy Scouts, Girl Guides and Boys' Brigades boasted a combined membership of more than two million children. They were sex-segregated and worked to delay any interest in the opposite sex. Instead they instilled ideals of discipline, deference to authority and patriotism. The big treat was the week away from home at the summer camp.

PUBERTY

But along with innocence went sexual ignorance and this could lead to problems. The majority of fifties children knew virtually nothing about the facts of life. At home any mention of sex was taboo. A Mass Observation survey in 1949 found that over 80 per cent of British children had received no sex education at all from their parents. Little changed in the fifties and it wasn't until the 1960s that sexual education was recognized as part of the school curriculum. In some schools children were taught to be ashamed of their sexuality. In convents, for example, girls often had to bath under a towel or wearing their pants and were told that it was a sin to look at their own bodies. As a consequence the onset of puberty could be traumatic, especially for girls. Some had no idea what was happening when their periods started. A few thought they were dying or that it was a punishment from God. More common was the experience of Jo Roffey from south London. 'When my periods started Mum told me to go straightaway to the shops and ask for some Dr White's. They were sanitary towels, but Mum was too embarrassed to say the actual words. When I got them she said I was to have nothing to do with boys from now on. Well blimey, that was confusing. I used to walk to school with the boys and play with them, I didn't know what to do. So I chatted to my girlfriends and found that some of them had started their periods too. You found out the little you knew from your girlfriends. Mum would never ever mention anything about sex to me.'

School DAYS

Schools embodied the paternalistic adult control that shaped childhood in the 1950s. The educational reforms of the immediate post-war years guaranteed an extended education for all and the school-leaving age was raised to fifteen. The standards of teachers were improved and there was greater investment in schools. But the classroom was permeated with traditions that found their inspiration in the Victorian public schools. For many grammar schools, there was a strict dress code that required boys to wear a blazer, cap and tie. The cane was inflicted frequently on both boys and girls. And the eleven-plus exam, introduced in the 1944 Education Act, selected eleven-year-old children into their appropriate secondary schools. Those who passed graduated to grammar school where they invariably received an excellent education. There was a lot at stake, as Linda Shanovitch remembers. 'My parents were frightfully middle class so it would have been a disaster not to pass the eleven-plus. I was terrified of failing. I remember on the day of the exam I got home and for a special treat my mother let me have fish fingers, which I was usually never allowed as she saw them as working-class food. All my friends were working class so I always wanted fish fingers. As it turned out I passed the exam and did really well, they said I was one of the cleverest girls in Islington.'

Those who failed – about 80 per cent of those who took the eleven-plus – were sent to local secondary modern schools. Despite all the official rhetoric, these provided an inferior education and many children who went to them – who were predominantly working class – were left with an abiding sense of failure. Some, like Jo Roffey, rebelled. 'I was the only girl in my junior school who failed the exam, so I had to go to the secondary modern. I was so embarrassed. And I didn't get on very well I'm afraid. I didn't take the lessons seriously. Once you get behind you're buggered really and I did get behind. At needlework I was terrible, it took me two years to make an apron. I couldn't see the point of French. All I wanted to do was muck about with the boys. I was always getting the cane, three on each hand, it didn't half hurt. They sent letters home to my mum and I'd throw them away because I didn't want to get into more trouble at home, did I? Then when I was fourteen they finally had enough. They expelled me.'

By the late fifties there was a growing realization that the system was wasteful and divisive. Opinion was shifting towards the comprehensive, non-selective secondary education that would transform state schooling in the next decade. The most dramatic changes in the sixties, though, began in infant and junior schools. These became increasingly child-centred, with opportunities for self-expression and creativity. Study trips and walks outside the school walls became an important part of the new way to learn. Inside school there was

A teacher tends to a crying boy in 1958. Schools – especially junior schools – began to be liberalised in the fifties and sixties.

also a more relaxed atmosphere. There were fewer rigid rules and far less corporal punishment. Children were encouraged to learn through play and develop their imaginations. New open-plan schools were built. Desks were in groups, not twos, and there was more freedom of movement.

LIVING *Dolls*

Sindy, the British answer to Barbie, first hit the market in 1963. Her boyfriend Paul was introduced two years later.

The sixties continued many of the trends of the previous decade, pushing Britain towards a more child-centred society. More money was spent on children. They were more indulged. And children's toys mirrored sixties fantasies and the new glamorous lifestyle that many aspired to. Nothing epitomized this more than Barbie, the American glamour doll who made her debut here in the early sixties. With her ever-expanding range of accessories and contemporary outfits, she quickly became established as the most popular toy for girls. In 1963 she was joined by her British-produced counterpart, Sindy, who was advertised as the 'the free, swinging, grown-up girl, who dresses the way she likes'. Her boyfriend Paul was introduced in 1965, and Patch, her little sister, a year later. Another import from the United States was Action Man. He arrived in 1966 and was for years one of the favourite toys for boys. Another big hit for sixties boys was Scalextric motor racing, which boasted cars that travelled at scale speeds of 130 miles an hour.

Many of the most popular toys were spin-offs from children's television series, reflecting the new importance of the medium in British life. Gerry Anderson's futuristic puppet series – *Stingray* (1964), *Thunderbirds* (1965) *Captain Scarlett and the Mysterons* (1967) and *Joe 90* (1968) – all spawned very popular merchandise. *Thunderbirds* star Lady Penelope with her pink Rolls-Royce, registration FAB 1, was a great favourite amongst girls. Clockwork Daleks and Astro ray Dalek guns were sold to millions of children on the back of the successful BBC series *Doctor Who*, which began in 1963. Then there were games linked to *The Magic Roundabout*, *Crackerjack*, *Huckleberry Hound*, *Basil Brush* and a host of other children's television series.

New PARENTING

In the sixties a new informal style of bringing up children was beginning to develop. Most child care was still the mother's responsibility but there were closer bonds with fathers than there had been earlier in the century. By the late 1960s increasing numbers of dads – most of them professional and middle class – wanted to be seen as friends rather than authority figures by their sons and daughters. The most daring even encouraged their children to call them by their Christian names, something unheard of in the past. Fathers came also to accept a slightly greater responsibility for the care of the children. This was in part due to economic changes. More and more married women were entering the job market in the sixties and dad was no longer the sole breadwinner as he had been in the early fifties. The clear and defined roles for mother and father were becoming blurred and many of them enjoyed their new role. As closer relationships developed within families, parents were less likely simply to lay down rules as they had in the past. More of them discussed with their children what they were doing, and explained why.

However, by the 1960s a new trend – that of divorce – began to undermine these more intimate bonds. During this decade the divorce rate more than doubled. Over half the marriages that ended involved children, more and more of whom had to contend with custody battles, long-running emotional tugs of war and step-parents on a scale that was unknown before the war. Some were left emotionally devastated.

'I was eight when Mum and Dad split up,' remembers Wendy Mitchell, who grew up in Bristol in the 1960s. 'Dad fell in love with another woman he met through work and he left home. Up until then everything had seemed so happy and I loved Dad so much, I was a real daddy's girl. That memory of him leaving is so painful I can't remember anything about it. I've blanked it out. And I can't remember anything about Dad being at home before then either, even though I know we did a lot of things together. The first effect it had on me was my school work. I couldn't concentrate, I'd sit staring out of the window. I couldn't believe it had happened. Every night when I said my prayers I used to say, "Please God, please make Mum and Dad get back together again, I'll do anything to make that happen." But it didn't. We saw Dad every Saturday and he'd take us out in his car to nice places and for walks, and buy me and my brother things. That was all great. Then when he brought us home I used to cry my eyes out. I used to say, "I want to be back with my dad." I feel so terrible now for Mum, I had no idea how hurtful it must have been for her. She was brilliant though, she never got upset with me and she never said a word against my dad to me. I really missed him, but the other thing was, looking back now I realize he was able to give us such a fun time. Mum didn't have any money and when we got home we had to help with all the chores and do our homework. Being with Dad was a wonderful escape from all that. What I'm most amazed about looking back, though, is how embarrassed and ashamed I was about Mum and Dad's divorce. I couldn't tell anyone about it. Not even my best friends. In those days divorce was still quite unusual and I wanted to be the same as everyone else. So for eight years I kept up the lie at school that Mum and Dad were still together. I never had friends back to the house because they might find something out. It all made me quite introverted. Then when I was sixteen I told one of my best friends. It was such a relief, it made me feel a lot better and only then did I really come to terms with what had happened.'

TWEENIES

The new sexual freedom that gave unhappy couples the opportunity to divorce also contributed to another big change that affected children's lives. This was the sexualization of childhood. It really began in the sixties, trickling down from the new youth culture that had been created by the rock 'n' roll generation. Children of eleven, twelve and thirteen now wanted their slice of the action. They wanted to dress fashionably and, in the case of girls, to wear make-up. They wanted to be more independent and have boyfriends and girlfriends like their older brothers and sisters. The new music and fashion industries increasingly saw children as a market for their sexualized products and reached them through the new pop music programmes on radio and television, and through teen magazines like *Jackie*, *Honey* and *Boyfriend*.

Young secondary-school boys and girls began spending much more time and money on their appearance. Girls in particular would spend hours preparing to go out on a Friday or Saturday night. The real devotees of fashion – most of them girls – no longer wanted to go rambling or hiking or join in competitive games. It was very uncool. And it might ruin their hairstyles, their make-up and their carefully groomed fingernails. Trish Hood from Bristol was thirteen in 1965. 'I was always getting into trouble at school over make-up and clothes and nail varnish. They used to want the girls to look prim and proper and be very plain but I just couldn't stand it. I remember once I was caught wearing nail varnish and I was taken into the chemistry laboratory and the teacher poured acid over my nails to get it off. It really hurt! What I hated most of all though, was going through the showers after our games lessons. I think the main reason was that it ruined my hairdo and wrecked my make-up. So I'd knock off. I'd just walk home when it was games lessons to get out of it.'

The battles with school authorities hotted up in the sixties. Eleven- and twelve-year- old girls wearing miniskirts and make-up became a regular bone of contention, and transistor radios were often banned on school premises. Leading pop groups like the Beatles and the Rolling Stones were greeted wherever they went by screaming, hysterical young schoolgirls. The girls were in love with their idols. It was a fantasy. But it was at least safer than actually having sex at a very young age. Surveys in the sixties discovered that children aged eleven, twelve, thirteen and fourteen were starting to be sexually active in greater numbers than ever before. Ignorance about contraception meant that unwanted pregnancies resulted. The problem of the schoolgirl mum hit the headlines and although it was greatly exaggerated – only a tiny minority of children at school was affected – it was a portent of things to come.

While the pressures to become sexual at a younger age could sometimes end in heartache and disaster, overall children's lives improved in the 1950s and 1960s. They grew up in an increasingly child-centred, comfortable and protected world and more of them could enjoy themselves free from the pressures of work and adult responsibilities. By the late sixties most children were enjoying rights and privileges, and a quality of life, that would have been undreamt of at the beginning of the twentieth century.

Girl, the popular teen magazine of the late fifties. Ten years later it was looking distinctly old-fashioned.

The best picture weekly for girls

The Scintillating **BSA SUNBEAM**

Teenage **Rebels**

I N THE 1960S BRITAIN WAS REVERED AS THE SWINGING capital of the world. London was at the epicentre of a huge explosion of youthful freedom. It was the home of hip, of the dedicated follower of fashion. As *Time* magazine put it in April 1966, 'in a decade dominated by youth, London has burst into bloom. It swings, it is the scene.' Within just two decades Britain had lost her empire but had discovered miniskirts, fashion boutiques, discos and the Beatles. The teenager – a word and a species unknown before the war – had shaken a deeply conservative nation to its foundations. Rebellious youth cults like beatniks, Teddy boys, mods, rockers and hippies had outraged their elders and betters. These were the years of the generation gap, when there was unprecedented conflict between young people and their parents.

Previous page The girl on a scooter, one of the emblematic images of the Swinging Sixties. Most sixties girls preferred to pose on them rather than ride them – it spoilt the hair.

> **"**
>
> THERE WERE NOTICES EVERYWHERE SAYING "NO JIVING OR BOPPING" AND THEY EVEN EMPLOYED A LOCAL HEAVY THAT WE CALLED RUBBER BELLY TO KEEP ORDER. WELL, ME AND MY GIRLFRIEND, WE WERE AMONGST THOSE WHO LOVED DOING ALL THE NEW ROCK AND ROLL ROUTINES, BUT THERE WERE LOTS OF OTHERS WHO JUST WANTED TO DO THE QUICKSTEP. WE WEREN'T GOING TO STOP, SO WHEN THE MUSIC STARTED HALF THE FLOOR ARE DOING THE QUICKSTEP AND THE OTHER HALF ARE JIVING.
>
> **"**

Jazz dancing in the late fifties. The early Jazz clubs were the cradle for the emerging teenage culture.

In this chapter we find out where this great surge of youthful creativity and independence came from. We chart the rise of teenagers to social and economic power in just two decades. We document the experience of ordinary ones and reveal how this changed between the early 1950s and late 1960s. This is the story of how the rock 'n' roll generation broke the mould of the old-fashioned, class-based society they grew up in just after the war. For the first time, young people developed their own music, their own identity and their own lifestyle. In so doing they made a lasting impact on the future of Britain.

In the early fifties there were few signs of the youthful explosion that was to emerge in the Swinging Sixties. Britain was a grey country dominated by austerity. Everything was rationed, from sweets to shoes. Clothes had to be bought with coupons saved over many months, and the more enterprising young women made their own dresses from curtain material. With goods in such short supply there was a flourishing black market in most items. On many street corners 'spivs' could be seen selling the most coveted of all articles: nylon stockings. Fashion-conscious girls who couldn't afford to buy them sometimes drew a simple black line up the back of each leg to give the appearance of nylons. For them, this was as far as style went. And any teenager who did try to look just a bit different often met public disapproval, as Pamela Woodland remembers. 'I was doing teacher training in Portsmouth and there it was acceptable to wear a hat at a jaunty angle on your head, covering your ears. Well, when I came home on holiday to Rotherham and I did this, you could hear all the tut-tuts as I walked through the town centre. This was quite something. But I wasn't daunted, I carried on wearing them.'

Style was essentially the preserve of the rich, as it had always been, and Britain's influences came from European cities, notably Paris with its haute couture. Even hairdressers had to adopt the style and mannerisms of the French if they wanted to be successful. During the early 1950s Raymond, the son of an Italian immigrant, born in Soho and later to be known as Mr Teasie-Weasie, took advantage of this in his high-class salons: 'Women at that time thought that the only good hairdressing could come from French hairdressers. So I taught stylists to use French expressions such as "Bonjour, madame", "Comment allez-vous, madame?" and all that nonsense. I also renamed them. If their name was Joe, I called them Louis or Monsieur Emile. They were all given a new name, French sounding.'

A camp-fire singsong in the early fifties – the final heyday of the Boy Scouts and the uniformed youth movement in Britain.

While the rich monopolized the world of fashion, the older generation imprinted itself on practically all the activities and entertainments available for young people. The early fifties witnessed the zenith of traditional values, old pastimes and adult authority. Church attendance rose. Membership of political parties increased. Youth organizations like the Boy Scouts prospered, boosted by the glamour of Britain's wartime triumphs. And family life flourished. The main entertainments were watching football, going to the cinema, rambling and cycling. Sometimes whole families would be involved – deprived of these simple pleasures during the war, they now resumed them with renewed vigour. Another legacy of the war was an enthusiasm for communal activities. In addition, lack of money meant that most people couldn't afford to do anything more grand.

The young found this post-war culture restricting and regimented. Fathers and elder brothers who had spent several years in the forces returned home and reasserted the old discipline that had been relaxed while they were away. The sexual permissiveness and loosening of moral standards that had been a feature of the war years also ended abruptly when family life resumed. Many dance halls had rules that tightly controlled the dress and behaviour of their customers and more adventurous dances like the jitterbug and the jive were banned in some places. 'I lived in a village in Staffordshire and every Saturday night I loved to go to the hop at the village hall,' says Graham Bill. 'There were notices everywhere saying "No Jiving or Bopping" and they even employed a local heavy that we called Rubber Belly to keep order. Well, me and my girlfriend, we were amongst those who loved doing all the new rock 'n' roll routines, but there were lots of others who just wanted to do the quickstep. We weren't going to stop, so when the music started half the floor are doing the quickstep and the other half are jiving. People were getting clouted round the ears with the flailing arms of the rock 'n' rollers. And if old Rubber Belly caught you he'd catch you by the scruff of the neck and march you out of the hall. "No jiving or bopping," he'd say. You wouldn't be let back in and sometimes you couldn't get in next week either.'

PEACETIME CONSCRIPTS

Young men at this time were confronted by the daunting prospect of National Service. Under the terms of the National Service Act of 1948 they were called up at the age of eighteen to undergo two years of military training and duty – the first time compulsory military service had been seen in Britain outside wartime. Many young fifties servicemen spent their entire term in draughty army barracks polishing boots and parade-bashing. Others were dispatched to the outposts of Britain's shrinking empire to fight her enemies. They took on left-wing guerrillas in the Malay jungle. In Kenya they tried to outwit the Mau Mau terrorists. They guarded the Suez Canal. And they went on desert forays in Aden and the troubled Gulf States. Around 400 were killed in action and many more were wounded. However, National Service was never a big political issue for British youth. Some young men actually enjoyed their service overseas as it opened up new horizons and experiences, just as it had for their fathers and brothers during the war. It was simply the conformity, the regimentation and the intense drabness of the post-war world they lived in that provided the spur for revolt.

New recruits square-bashing in February 1953. National Service became unpopular with the new breed of teenager – and was abolished in 1960.

ALL *that* JAZZ

The revolt began in Soho. An underground culture developed there that paved the way for the area that was later to become the heart of Swinging London. The driving forces were jazz and marijuana. By the early fifties, jazz basement clubs like Ronnie Scott's Club 11 honeycombed the streets of Soho and there were all-night sessions of trad and modern jazz featuring artists like the young George Melly. At the same time, new all-night coffee bars became established in the area. Serving Italian-style espresso coffee and providing a jukebox or live music, they acquired a powerful mystique as oases of alternative culture. The first to open was the Moka in Frith Street in 1952, but it was quickly surpassed in fashionability by the Heaven and Hell in Old Compton Street.

BEATNIKS *and* BEARDS

The coffee bars and jazz clubs acted as a magnet for the first-ever British youth cult of the post-war years: the beats or beatniks, as its followers came to be known. Most were young and middle class, often aspiring actors, artists, designers or students, and because there were so many of them in London Soho was at the heart of the beatnik culture. Helped by outraged articles in the popular press, the new cult spread all over Britain, inspired by the American beat generation and by the beat authors and poets Jack Kerouac and Allen Ginsberg. Its philosophy was existentialist. Beatniks valued spontaneity, creativity and anything unconventional. The buzzword was to be cool. But there was also a political edge to this subculture. In the late 1950s it provided strong support for the first Ban the Bomb marches from Aldermaston to London, and the Trafalgar Square demonstrations of the early Campaign for Nuclear Disarmament. In fact, for many people it was the imminent threat of a holocaust and a sense of futility about the future that was their raison d'être for becoming a beat. 'I just couldn't stand the look of the life in front of me,' says Dixie Dean from north London, a beatnik of the early fifties. 'I knew the world was coming to an end. The nuclear holocaust was very real and we knew it was going to happen. The pictures that came out of Hiroshima and Nagasaki that we saw were deeply traumatizing. I was offered a scholarship to Cambridge University, which was pretty special then, but I turned it down. What was the point when we were all going to die? Our parents couldn't understand us because we were really the first teenagers to reject society. We

IS THIS JUST ANOTHER FAD?

The big beret.

12s 6d.

12 Quant colours.

Enquiries for Quant Berets
30 Fitzroy
Square,
London W1.

MARY QUANT

certainly couldn't be bothered to explain to them what we were feeling.'

The beatnik style was the first big fashion rebellion of teenagers. Its elements were shapeless jumpers, polo-necked sweaters, duffel coats and sandals; the predominant colour was black. Girls often had long straggly hair and wore lots of white make-up and dark eyeliner. Many men grew beards, a symbol of their rejection of the square, clean-cut world of military-style conformity that they loathed. But when beatniks were called up for National Service the sergeant majors could take their revenge. 'I knew the beard would have to go, that was the first thing they told me, they thought this was great,' remembers Dixie Dean, who began his service with the RAF in 1956. 'I cared about my beard, it was my beat symbol, it was what made me me and not one of them. I said "I'll shave it off myself." "No you won't, we'll

do it." And we had a row and I was in trouble. That was my first day. They did shave my beard off and I felt I'd lost a bit of me. My National Service was absolute hell. I realize now that the men who were training me were trying to make sure we had no will of our own, they were crushing all independence. But that was the last thing you could do to a beat. They couldn't knock it out of me and the first thing I did when I left was to join one of the CND marches from Aldermaston to Trafalgar Square.' Dixie later went on to an alternative career in academia and became a university professor.

Although most beatniks were anti-style, and enjoyed shocking the respectable with their unkempt, scruffy appearance, in their ranks there was a more fashion-conscious and life-affirming element who loved to wear colourful clothes, especially for jazz dancing. Some of these young rebels would later rise to fame in the London fashion world of the sixties. One was a former art student at Goldsmith's College: Mary Quant. 'I hated the clothes the way they were so I used to make circular skirts out of marvellous great prints and find black tights from theatrical costumiers and black ballet shoes and black leotard tops, and these skirts were really great to dance in. What I loathed was the unsexiness, the lack of gaiety, the formal stuffiness of the

Many of the sixties fashion gurus like Mary Quant were former art students and beatniks.

39

look that was said to be fashion. I wanted clothes that were much more for life, much more for real people, much more for being young and alive in.'

In 1955 Quant opened Bazaar, London's first boutique. Located in Chelsea's King's Road, its distinctive feature was its free and easy atmosphere which allowed customers to browse and try on clothes unattended – a sharp contrast to the formal ways of established clothes shops. All the designs were by Quant. Within a few years similar boutiques were sprouting up nearby. Chelsea was becoming trendy. Bazaar provided the model for the new kind of fashion and shopping that was at the heart of Swinging London ten years later.

TEDDY BOYS

The Teddy Boys first emerged in south London in the early fifties. They epitomised the new teenage narcissism – their most treasured possession was not the flick-knife but the comb.

Another youth cult was emerging at this time: the Teddy boys. Like that of the beatniks, it also began in London, but whereas beats were predominantly middle class, the Teddy boys were overwhelmingly from working-class backgrounds. Their name was first coined in the early fifties as a derogatory reference to south London teenagers who 'took over' the latest style for the rich – Savile Row was attempting to relaunch the 'look' of the Edwardian dandy for young aristocratic men about town. The Teddy boys adopted the draped jackets and velvet collars of this fashion and combined them with

drainpipe trousers, or jeans and bootlace ties which they had seen American cowboys wearing in films. This was to be their distinctive uniform.

The Teds liked fighting and there were many reported confrontations with the police, with National Servicemen and between rival gangs of Teddy boys. Many of the fights were over girls. 'Nine times out of ten the trouble started over a girl,' says Mick Johns from Tunbridge Wells. 'You'd get two gangs of Teds at a dance and somebody would fancy somebody else's girlfriend. I always went tooled up. I'd have a bicycle chain and fish hooks behind my lapels so that if someone grabbed hold of me they'd get stuck and I could just bang them. That never happened with me, but it could get nasty.'

Although the press associated Teds with gang violence, their most treasured possession was not the flick knife but the comb. They were extremely narcissistic and the worst violence often arose when they overreacted to insults about their dress. The first murder by a Teddy boy, on Clapham Common in 1953, occurred when a youth taunted one of them with the words 'flash cunt'. A well-groomed quiff and Brylcreemed hair added the finishing touches to the slick image the Teds were cultivating. Traditional 'bob a knob' barbers whose repertoires were limited to a short back and sides had to adapt quickly to the changing fashion. Brian Fleiss, an early Teddy Boy in Burnt Oak, north London, remembers: 'You used to go in and ask for a Tony Curtis and get the barber to put a quiff on the front. I'd tell him I wanted plenty on the front.'

Most parents strongly opposed the idea of their sons becoming Teds. The backlash was especially strong in the north, where it was seen as an effeminate, antisocial, southerners' craze. Some fathers forbade their boys wearing Teddy boy clothes, but there were always devious ways around this prohibition. 'Darlington was a very conservative place in the fifties, where fathers ruled the roost,' says Ray Pratt. 'I wanted to be a Teddy boy, they were the thing, it was the outrage of the time, but my father was very strict and he thought it was disgusting, they should all be locked up. So I had to do it secretly. I bought my Teddy boy suit in bits and pieces. But I never wore it in the house, I kept it at my mate's house, his parents were more easy-going. My dad would have given me a good hiding and thrown me out. And there was nowhere to go then, young people couldn't get flats by themselves, that didn't happen. When I went out I wore my flannels and everyday clothes, went round to my mate's house, put my Teddy boy suit on, out we went, then change and home by ten. No later or there would have been trouble.'

ROCK *'n'* ROLL

Once again, the driving force behind the new youth cult was music. But while the beatniks raved about jazz, the Teddy boys were devoted followers of the rock 'n' roll music that was arriving from the United States. It featured the electric guitar and was loud, brash and aggressive. It became the music of choice of the young generation. To the old this new music seemed discordant and disturbing, and dangerously sexual. But the explosive sounds of Elvis Presley and Bill Haley captured the mood of the young, and their yearning for freedom and excitement. Elvis, with his curled lip and pelvic thrusts, confirmed the worst fears of parents. He first entered the top ten in May 1956 (the charts had been invented the previous year) and within six months he had six smash hits: 'Heartbreak Hotel', 'Blue Suede Shoes', 'Hound Dog', 'Don't be Cruel', 'Blue Moon' and 'Love Me Tender'. Elsie Murphy from Liverpool was a fan. 'Elvis wasn't allowed to be shown below the waist because the adults were worried about his influence on us. At school we were allowed to bring in our own records for the last day of term, but there was a ban on Elvis. You could have Pat Boone but you couldn't have Elvis.'

The first teenage heroes were American, none more so than rock icon Elvis Presley. But there was soon a stream of home-grown British imitators like Cliff Richard and Billy Fury.

Haley, with a curious kiss curl on his forehead and in his thirties by the time he became famous, was not an obvious rock idol in the Elvis mould. But in 1956 his film *Rock Around the Clock* created pandemonium in British cinemas. In a mood of euphoria Teddy boys and girls danced in the aisles and slashed cinema seats. The Teds had a passion for jiving and after leaving the cinemas they jived through the streets, holding up traffic. In Oxford Street, despite police reinforcements, the mass dancing spread to the bonnets of parked cars. In Bootle, a thousand dancing Teds were shepherded through the town centre by baton-waving police. The teenage mayhem even reached the small mill town of Colne in Lancashire. 'I was a Teddy boy then and we all went a bit daft in the cinema,' says Dave Palmer. 'It was a great atmosphere and everybody was jiving in the aisles. And we started doing things we shouldn't have done. We were tearing seats off, ripping off covers and throwing stuff into the air. And they said that's it, everybody out and they closed the cinema down. It was just too exciting for words.'

The beatniks and Teddy boys were pioneers, breaking new ground and flouting convention. They had raised the spectre of teenagers with their own style and culture. The subject was much debated in the press, and rock 'n' roll struck terror into the heart of Middle England. Although only a small minority of young people had actually embraced the cults, the rebellion gained some momentum in the mid- to late fifties. There were home-grown rock 'n' roll performers, many of whom began their careers at the 2 i's coffee bar in Soho. Amongst the best known were Tommy Hicks (stage name Tommy Steele), Harry Webb (Cliff Richard) and Terry Nelhams (Adam Faith). These and other early pop artists were showcased in television shows like the BBC's *Juke Box Jury*, introduced by David Jacobs, and *Six-Five Special*, hosted by Pete Murray. But it was all pretty tame stuff. As the beatniks and Teddy boys settled down and got married there was a vacuum. With a new decade beginning, young people were searching for something different, something that felt theirs, something more exciting.

The YOUTHQUAKE

The real youth explosion was about to begin, rooted in the growing confidence and affluence of the young generation. Wages had been gradually improving since the early fifties, but it was in the period between 1958 and 1966 that young people really enjoyed the fruits of affluence. During this time their income almost doubled in real terms. Added to this, most families were now so much better off that there was a breakdown of the old tradition of teenage sons and daughters handing over most of their wages to their parents to help pay the bills. For the first time ever, the young were economically independent and had a substantial amount of disposable income. In the early 1960s the average wage of teenagers was around £10 a week. Of this about £7 was left as disposable income after they had paid their keep at home. Their spending power was increased by the rapid spread of hire purchase from the late fifties onwards. And the economic importance of youth was heightened by the fact that in the early sixties almost 40 per cent of the population was under twenty-five. The post-war baby boom meant that Britain was a young country and

> WE STARTED DOING THINGS WE SHOULDN'T HAVE DONE. WE WERE TEARING SEATS OFF, RIPPING OFF COVERS AND THROWING STUFF INTO THE AIR. AND THEY SAID THAT'S IT, EVERYBODY OUT AND THEY CLOSED THE CINEMA DOWN. IT WAS JUST TOO EXCITING FOR WORDS.

The pouting and posing Mick Jagger and the Rolling Stones brought a new sexual aggression to the British pop scene in the early sixties.

youth suddenly became a very lucrative market. There was a boom in record buying with sales of singles climbing between 1960 and 1965. 'Every week I'd buy at least two or three new singles. I wish I'd kept them, they'd be worth a fortune now,' says Dave Gregory, from Coventry. 'I had so much money to spend, it's unbelievable looking back. There were so many well-paid jobs for teenagers connected with the car industry. I'd spend ten pounds every weekend on myself, on clothes, on going out and, most of all, on music.'

Young people also had more free time than ever before as the number of hours spent at work gradually reduced. Holidays with pay were increasing. Labour-saving innovations in the home, like washing machines, vacuum cleaners and convenience foods also created more free time, especially for girls who had once been tied to the kitchen sink. And in 1960 National Service, which had deprived most teenage boys of two years of freedom, was abolished.

There was a huge market eager to buy into a new, independent and rebellious teenage lifestyle. But the older generation who dominated the worlds of music and fashion were completely out of touch with what it wanted. It was the young themselves who had their finger on the pulse. They were to provide the musicians, artists, designers and entrepreneurs of all sorts who would create the Swinging Sixties scene. Many of the leading figures came from a working-class background and had gone to art college – the beneficiaries of the 1944 Education Act that had extended educational opportunities for all. Countless pioneers of pop music like John Lennon and Paul McCartney, Ray Davies of the Kinks, Pete Townsend of the Who and Keith Richards of the Rolling Stones had been to art school.

MERSEYBEAT

Music was at the heart of the youth explosion. The inspiration came not just from rock 'n' roll, and jazz – by the early sixties there was a growing interest in other styles like Delta blues, electric rhythm and blues and soul. This kind of music was hardly played or produced in Britain and had to be imported, usually through records made by obscure American companies. Liverpool, with its direct shipping route to the United States, was one of the best places to get hold of these records, one of many reasons why it quickly became the musical capital of Britain. The music of the Beatles, the greatest pop group of all time, was a fusion of these influences. They sold millions of records and conquered America, which had dominated popular music for much of the twentieth century. They wrote all their own songs and performed them live.

Jackie was one of a new breed of teenage magazine that helped promote new pop idols and encouraged the cult of fan worship in the sixties.

The response was Beatlemania, with screaming, fainting fans greeting their every appearance. Within a few years they were, as John Lennon put it, more famous than Jesus Christ. But Liverpool was not just famous for the Beatles. It also produced Cilla Black, the Searchers, Gerry and the Pacemakers, Billy J Kramer, the Swinging Blue Jeans and more than 300 other professional or semi-professional bands. The Merseybeat was first heard at the Cavern, a converted warehouse basement, which soon became the most talked about and influential club in Britain.

Each city had its own bands, many of them with a loyal following. Music offered an alternative career, a way out of boring office and factory jobs, and thousands dreamt of fame and fortune. Most big cities produced at least one or two successful bands in the sixties. Herman's Hermits and the Hollies came out of Manchester, the Animals from Newcastle and the Spencer Davis Group, the Move and the Moody Blues from Birmingham. London also produced a

crop of leading bands, rivalling the musical dominance of Liverpool. There were the Rolling Stones, the Who, the Kinks, the Yardbirds, the Pretty Things and the East End's very own Small Faces. In the early years, before they became big celebrities, many of the band members remained close to their fans and would drink and dance with them after gigs. This easy access to the bands gave some young teenagers illusions of romance – as Dorothy Robson remembers. 'We loved Herman's Hermits, they were local to Accrington where we lived and they played a lot there. We'd go backstage and we'd chat them up after they'd played. And I remember they had a hit called "Mrs Brown You've Got a Lovely Daughter". Well my friend Linda, she was Linda Brown, and she was absolutely convinced that this record was written for her. We were only fourteen. "Oh, he's singing my song." It was pathetic!'

For every band that made it into the big time there were fifty that didn't. One of the up-and-coming young rock 'n' roll bands in Bristol during the early sixties was Mike Tobin and the Magnettes. 'A lot of the bands were calling themselves after American cars like the Cadillacs, so being grammar-school boys we thought we'd be a bit posh and name ourselves after a British sports car, the Magnette,' Mike Tobin remembers. 'How pretentious can you get. Well, in Bristol alone there were about 300 rock bands playing at that time. They all had followings because it was a long way to go to London then, there were no discos and there was not much pop music on the television or the radio. We had a big crowd of girls who'd follow us wherever we played and they would scream, just like they did with Elvis. Yes, everybody got screamed at. We certainly did. And we had dreams of stardom. But what was our undoing, we all ended up marrying our most avid fans. And once we were married the first thing they wanted us to do was to pack the band in, because now they'd got us they didn't want to share us with anybody else.'

DISCO FEVER

Soon all bands had to compete with the new discos. The first, spawned in London, was La Discotheque, the first club to play records as opposed to featuring live bands. By the mid-sixties the fashion for discos with disc jockeys had spread not only throughout London but across Britain. Some of the clubs stayed open all night and to keep dancing the most dedicated pleasure-seekers took amphetamines. These were then within the law – the pills, known to the initiated as purple hearts, French blues or black bombers could be obtained on prescription or bought for a few pence at many discos and clubs.

The MOD

The clothes the boutiques were selling in the early sixties were modernist or mod, the latest youth cult to hit Britain. This, too, began in London. Mods were much more smooth and sophisticated than the Teds and beatniks. Mod boys – most of whom were young apprentices and office workers – spent most of their money on clothes. They wore impeccable Italian suits with narrow lapels, tailor-made for them, handmade winkle-picker shoes and shirts with pointed collars. The image was completed with a short neat Italian or French hairstyle. Mods wore parkas – all-weather cape-shaped coats – to protect their clothes and keep them clean and tidy while they were bombing around town on their Italian Lambretta or Vespa motor scooters. They were into money and style. Most of them would have preferred an E-Type Jag, but as they didn't have the cash they made do with scooters which were

Carnaby Street was the epicentre of the fashion scene in the sixties.

Swinging London in 1966. By then the clothes worn by teenagers and twenty-somethings had been changed for ever.

beautifully adorned and personalized. For a mod girl like Dorothy Robson from Lancashire, the quality of the scooter was vitally important when choosing a boyfriend. 'It didn't matter what he looked like as long as he didn't look like what we called a pie crust. As long as he had a flashy scooter with all the gear we went out with him and that was that.'

Mods could indulge their taste for smart clothes as never before in the boutiques, most of which were in Chelsea's King's Road, or in Carnaby Street in Soho, where they were mostly for men. The male vanity inherent in the mod style meant that the latter represented a big slice of the market. By the early sixties half a dozen boutiques in this Soho back street were owned by one man. John Stephen, a Glaswegian grocer's son, had come to London in 1956 when he was nineteen and had carefully observed what the mod fashion leaders, known as 'faces', were wearing and what they wanted. The moment a new style appeared on the streets he made it available in his boutiques. All the latest mod trends like mohair suits or white suits were anticipated and catered for by Stephen – he also sold hipsters in a range of bright colours which, until then, few men had dared wear for fear of being thought to be gay. While the early mods had had to get their clothes made to measure from tailors, most of the new boutique ones were off the peg – and a lot cheaper. Stephen's chain of boutiques spread throughout Britain and then the world. And there were a hundred imitators. The clothes worn by fashionable teenagers and twenty-somethings had been changed for ever. Young men became peacocks, and as their confidence grew the styles they wore became more extravagant – frilly and foppish with bright, flowery shirts, big collars, chiffon scarves and patterned waistcoats.

Fashion REVOLUTION

If Liverpool led the music scene then London was undeniably the fashion capital for teenagers. Boutiques, following Mary Quant's prototype, spread all over the capital – by the mid-sixties there were more than 1500 in Greater London alone. They were small, informal and friendly, and often sold clothes made by their owners, who had recently graduated from art school. With speakers fixed to the walls, music would be blasted into the customers' ears, adding to the atmosphere. Shopping had never been like this before. One of the most fashionable sixties boutiques was Biba, founded by designer Barbara Hulanicki who opened her first shop in Kensington in 1964. She hired the so-called Biba twins, Rosie and Susie, who, though only shop assistants, became minor celebrities in their own right. 'Every Saturday it was madness,' remembers Biba twin Rosie Young. 'It was an amazing atmosphere, there were hundreds of girls milling around the shop. You just couldn't move. The changing rooms were knee-deep in clothes. Nobody put anything back. All the clothes were so cheap, you wore them one week and threw them away the next. That didn't stop lots of the gear being pinched. Hardly anybody came in without buying something or taking it. It was so chaotic, there were bags everywhere. Once the morning's takings were handed over to one of the customers in a bag, instead of her feather boa. Nobody noticed at the time.'

The girls weren't going to be left out of this fashion revolution. There was a new approach to dress described by Harper's Bazaar in 1966 as 'enjoy-it-today-sling-it-tomorrow'. That was precisely what was done with paper dresses, which enjoyed a brief vogue. New materials like Melinex, lurex and PVC mirrored the new technology and excitement of the space age and geometric shapes became fashionable. The high priestess of the new look for girls was Mary Quant and her boutique, Bazaar. Hers was the look adopted by most mod girls. She majored in simple, bright designs and is credited with the invention of the most famous of all 1960s fashions: the miniskirt. By the mid-sixties a million of these had been sold in boutiques and department stores throughout the land. Worn with tights, the miniskirt became the defining look of the decade – and more than any other fashion it captured the sixties mood of teenage sexual confidence and freedom.

But wearing one wasn't without its problems. Though the miniskirt was designed to be eye-catching, girls found they were sometimes attracting the wrong sort of attention, especially when getting in and out of cars or on to buses. Helen Hackney from Chester remembers: 'If you were waiting at a bus stop in a miniskirt and you were behind a man in the queue he'd often wave you in front as though he was being a gentleman. Then he'd follow you upstairs to look up your skirt. I used to have to virtually go up the stairs sideways or backwards and then sit with my handbag on my knees.' In offices many dolly-bird secretaries complained that men were ogling their legs and looking up their skirts as they sat at the new open-fronted desks that were fashionable in the sixties. A protective panel called the 'modesty board' came into vogue as a result. Val Hill remembers how important they were to London's young female office workers. 'It became one of the perks of the job. You not only asked for a rather good salary and an electric typewriter, but also a modesty board. And if there were no modesty boards then you might renegotiate the salary.'

The fashion explosion helped to fuel a boom in hairdressing. Following in the slipstream of Mary Quant's success was hairdresser Vidal Sassoon. An East End boy who had served his apprenticeship under leading stylist Mr Teasie-Weasie, Sassoon disliked the grand and elaborate styles popular in the fifties and developed a much more natural style, the geometric cut, in his Bond Street salon. This perfectly complemented the unfussy clothes Quant was designing and set the trend for young people.

The ROCKERS

By the mid-sixties as many as a third of teenage boys and girls regarded themselves as mods, even if it only meant that they wore a sharp suit or a miniskirt. But they now had a rival and a sworn enemy: the rockers. Macho and mostly working class, and often the younger brothers of Teddy boys, rockers had long greasy hair, leather jackets and tattoos. They were obsessed with motorbikes and their power and speed and were the ton-up boys on the new motorways. Their heroes were the American Hell's Angels. Rockers congregated at petrol-station cafes like the Ace and the Busy Bee around the Watford end of the M1. They despised mods and loved to burn them up on their bigger, faster bikes. They saw mods as sad people because they were so soft and effeminate. 'He looks so pretty I almost fancy him myself' was the stock way to put down a young mod dressed up to the nines. Life for rockers was all about danger and risk-taking on the roads, and many died or were disabled for the cause. Their rebellion was very different to that of the mods but, though anti-style, it was another expression of sixties teenage affluence and independence.

The FIFTIES and SIXTIES

The mods, for their part, despised the rockers. Usually, though, they ignored them. But in 1964, on a cold wet Easter weekend at Clacton-on-Sea, 1000 mods caused mayhem when they fought with rockers amongst the stacked-up deckchairs. For the next two years there would be ritual battles every summer bank holiday on the beaches of south coast seaside resorts like Margate, Brighton, Bournemouth and Hastings. Most of the combatants drove down from London, desperate for some action and excitement to break up a boring weekend. Hundreds were fined and a few imprisoned. Local magistrates spoke of 'filth', 'pollution' and 'sawdust Caesars'. However, the violence and destruction of property was greatly exaggerated by a sensation-seeking press. One of those involved was Terry Shanahan, then a young north London mod. 'They called them battles, but believe me there wasn't much violence. It was all tribal posturing. It started on the way down, we'd be on our Lambrettas and they'd overtake us on their BSAs, because we were flat out at 65 mph and they'd do over a ton. When they overtook some would give you some stick. "What's that you're driving, a lawnmower or a sewing machine," that sort of thing. Down there, we were much sharper in appearance and they were greasy and unkempt so we'd go for them. "You greasy lump of shit, you've got a bag of chips on your head, you slimy-looking rat. And what's that with you, is it a female?" Well, that rocker girl didn't like that. They couldn't take that, that's what really started the trouble. There was a lot of running around, a few slaps, a few got a good kicking and maybe a few lumps. It wasn't much more than that. You spent most of the day running around, you were knackered. You felt you'd been in a fight but often you hadn't.'

The Ace Café in June 1962. This was the most fashionable haunt in the land for leather-clad rockers on the look out for a burn up.

SWINGING LONDON

While politicians argued over the moral decline of modern British youth, the mod style of Swinging London was becoming high fashion. It was sold through new magazines like the *Sunday Times* colour supplement, which began in 1962. Fashion modelling and photography were transformed from the rather mundane jobs they had been into glamorous and lucrative careers. Three of the most celebrated photographers at this time were David Bailey, Terence Donovan and Brian Duffy, all of whom were East End born and bred. One of the most famous models of the era was Lesley Hornby, better known as Twiggy, who was launched into stardom as 'the face of 1966' a few weeks before sitting her 'O' levels at Neasden High School for Girls.

Soon the smart metropolitan set was adopting the fashions of the young generation and mingling with its stars. New exclusive London clubs like the Ad Lib and the Cromwellian opened. Heirs and heiresses rubbed shoulders with aristocrats of the pop and fashion world like Mick Jagger, Mary Quant and top model Jean Shrimpton. Together they formed a young jet set whose private lives filled the gossip columns of every newspaper. The image of young working-class men and women who'd made it to the top mixing with the old rich fed the myth that Swinging London was classless. It was an illusion. In fact, many young people came to strongly dislike the obsession with money, material success and modernity that this new super-elite represented.

Twiggy, the cover girl of *Woman* magazine in August 1967. She had been launched into sixties stardom the previous year before sitting her 'O' levels at Neasden High School for Girls.

The SUMMER *of* LOVE

The swinging London scene and the mod style that had helped to shape it lost their ascendancy and went into decline after 1966. A new youth cult was emerging: the hippies. Its source of inspiration was the counterculture in California and it revolved around heavy rock music, drugs, mysticism, communal living and political dissent. Its popularity was in part a reaction against the commercialization of the Mod style. The hippie movement took off in Britain during 1967, the Summer

of Love, and influenced young people for the rest of the sixties. It appealed largely to middle-class youth, especially to sixth-formers and university students. There were 'be-ins', 'happenings' and open-air rock concerts, the largest of which was the Isle of Wight festival of 1969. The music was increasingly experimental and the Beatles' 'Sgt Pepper's Lonely Hearts Club Band' became the ultimate hippie album. These were the years of progressive and sometimes pretentious rock music, with Jimi Hendrix and Eric Clapton the two great guitar heroes. Young hippies wanted to expand their minds and used drugs like marijuana and LSD to achieve this. A few dropped out to live in free-love communes, most of which were doomed to failure. It was a movement that was easily parodied. But its ideals of peace, love and gentleness, and its open attitude to other cultures, were positive influences. They would have a deep and lasting effect on many of those who embraced them.

The world of the teenager in the late sixties was unrecognizable compared to the early fifties. The youth of Britain had discovered a new and independent identity. They had their own music, their own fashions and their own culture. They had helped to create industries that reflected their interests and tastes, and in which they could pursue alternative careers as musicians, designers and pop entrepreneurs. Teenagers wore what they wanted, when they wanted. In the war between the generations there was no doubt who were the winners and the losers.

The Summer of Love in 1967, a time of 'be-ins', 'happenings' and open-air rock concerts.

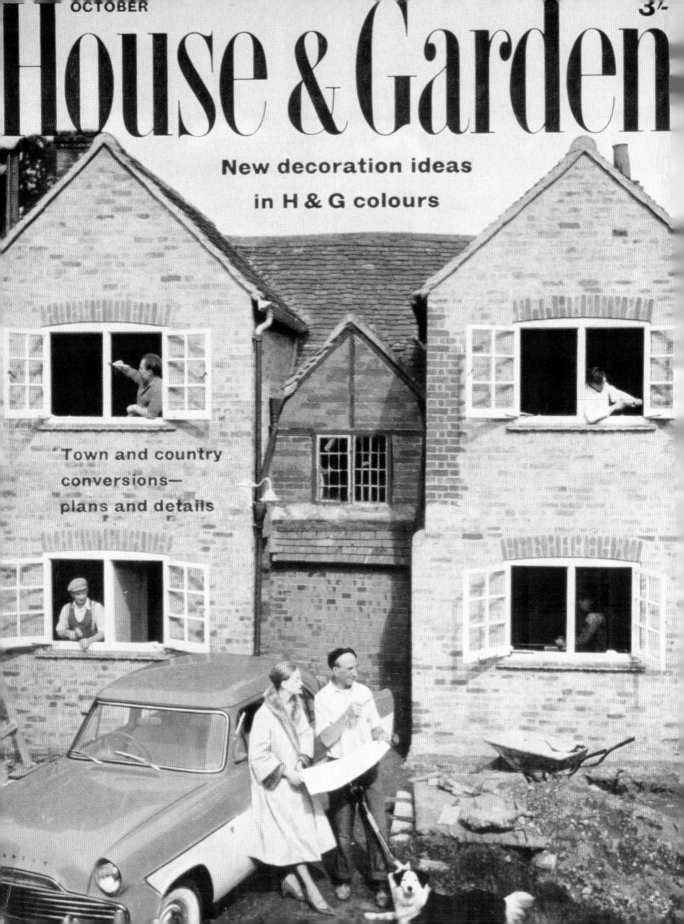

OCTOBER

House & Garden

3/-

New decoration ideas
in H & G colours

'Town and country
conversions—
plans and details

Dream **Homes**

I N THE SUMMER OF 1951 MILLIONS OF PEOPLE VISITED THE Festival of Britain, a government-sponsored extravaganza on the south bank of the Thames in London. On 27 acres of bomb-scarred wasteland some of the best architects in the country had built a miniature wonderland, a vision of the new Britain that would rise out of the ashes of war. Visitors were entranced by modern designs like the Dome of Discovery and the Skylon. Buses ferried them to the Exhibition of Living Architecture in the East End. Here, a new neighbourhood was being built to replace the bombed Victorian terraces of Poplar. Named after George Lansbury, the famous leader of the Labour Party who had been a councillor for the borough, it represented an idealistic vision of the city of the future. The standards of comfort and convenience were higher than ever before. It was a showcase of the better world the nation had fought for. The first residents couldn't believe their luck – after enduring damp, bug-infested, overcrowded, bomb-damaged homes, this was paradise.

Previous page The affluent younger generation didn't want to rent from a landlord or the council. They wanted a home of their own – preferably brand new.

The grand scheme of the new generation of planners and architects in the fifties and sixties was to build a better Britain. In the vanguard of a post-war housing revolution, they masterminded the clearance of great swathes of old Victorian cities and aimed to replace them with modern council homes. However, during these decades a new dream was emerging: home-ownership. The more affluent younger generation aspired to a home of their own and this began to shape the modern ideal of married life. Couples moved out to the new suburbs, the traditional haven for home-owners, and some by the late sixties had become more adventurous and began gentrifying country cottages and grand run-down properties in the Victorian suburbs of cities. By the late sixties, the new dream of a nation of home-owners was beginning to replace the old ideal of decent public housing for all.

Bombed OUT

In the immediate post-war years Britain faced a severe housing crisis. The Luftwaffe had destroyed almost half a million homes, leaving huge tracts of bomb-shattered wasteland in badly hit cities like London, Liverpool, Glasgow, Bristol and Plymouth. In Stepney in London's East End, for example, the Blitz had demolished one-third of all the houses or made them uninhabitable. Even before the war there had been a shortage of decent housing, but now the combined effects of bomb damage, a flood of returning soldiers and the baby boom made the lack of homes a desperate problem for the government. Most official estimates admitted a shortage of around four million homes, and over a quarter of a million families were forced to live in buildings that were unfit for human habitation. Many were newly marrieds who lived with relatives or in cramped furnished rooms. For several years after the war Gina Spreckley lived in north London with her husband and two small children. 'We had rooms in a house belonging to a relative. We only took it because there was nothing else. The whole house was crumbling. Every time you shut a door hard a bit of the ceiling fell down. Big mushrooms the size of breakfast plates grew up the walls, and if you cut them down in a few days they grew back again. There was a hole in the bedroom floor a foot square where the rats had gnawed away. My daughter had asthma because of the conditions. And we had no privacy, no bathroom of our own. What there was we had to share with all the other tenants. We couldn't report it to the health authorities because it belonged to a relative and we were just grateful to have a roof over our heads. It made me so depressed that I became suicidal, I felt I couldn't go on.'

BETTER HOMES *for All*

But there was hope. This was a time of optimism and idealism born out of the shared sacrifice of the war and ambitious government plans aimed to build five million homes in the next ten years. The determination to provide better housing for all shaped many of the new housing developments in the 1950s and 1960s. But it was always going to be difficult. At the end of the Second World War around 60 per cent of the population still lived in private rented accommodation characterized by lack of repairs, lack of investment and exploitative landlords. The poorest conditions were in working-class areas where there was often no hot running water or inside toilet or bathroom. Returning servicemen were angry at the terrible housing conditions they had to begin family life in. 'I'd fought, with everyone else, for a better world and I wanted a decent home to bring my children up in,' says David Ritchie from Dundee. 'What we got when I came out of the army was

In the fifties and sixties ambitious slum clearance schemes led to the mass demolition of Victorian terraces and tenements in inner city areas.

a bug-infested tenement that was no better than what I'd known as a child myself in the Depression years. Our children were being bitten by these bugs, there were mice everywhere and there was the constant smell of the shared toilets and blocked drains. It was absolutely terrible.'

The idealistic post-war Labour government had tried to tackle this problem by building new council estates, controlled by local authorities, on the outskirts of cities. These followed the example of the suburban homes for heroes built after the First World War, but this time the heroes' homes were better. There were generous-sized rooms, big windows and gardens, all designed to deliver a healthier, happier society. Health minister Aneurin Bevan even insisted on a downstairs as well as an upstairs toilet. One of the most ambitious local authorities was the London County Council, which built huge out-of-town council estates like Oxhey and Borehamwood in Hertfordshire and Debden and Harold Hill in Essex.

> "
> I WENT DOWN TO DUNDEE CORPORATION TO PUT MY NAME DOWN FOR A HOUSE. THEY TOOK ALL THE DETAILS AND I ASKED WHEN I MIGHT EXPECT TO GET A HOUSE. THE MAN SAID THAT WHERE YOU ARE ON THE LIST, IF YOU COME BACK IN FIFTEEN YEARS, WE'LL SEE HOW WE'RE GETTING ON.
> "

Local authority housing offices were besieged by queues of families looking to escape from the slums. However, lack of money and building materials meant that government building fell far short of its targets. Bevan's insistence that the new houses should be of the highest quality meant that fewer could be afforded. The building of a quarter of a million small, cheap 'prefabs' – made from prefabricated sections – helped to boost the numbers but there was still a big shortfall. In all, around one million new homes had been built by the Labour government by 1951. There were still millions of people desperate to get away from slum landlords. In 1951, the average waiting time for a family to obtain a council home in London was eight to ten years. In some cities it was even longer. 'I went down to Dundee Corporation to put my name down for a house,' says David Ritchie. 'They took all the details and I asked when I might expect to get a house. The man said that where you are on the list, if you come back in fifteen years, we'll see how we're getting on.'

Some people would find homes and jobs in the new towns, the brainchild of architect Patrick Abercrombie. In 1944 he had drafted the Greater London plan, one of the few idealistic wartime planning schemes ever to be realized. He proposed that 300,000 people should be moved out of inner London into a ring of eight new towns. These were constructed in the post-war years beyond a green belt and formed a ring around London. The eight were Stevenage, Hatfield, Hemel Hempstead and an extended Welwyn Garden City in

Hertfordshire; Bracknell in Berkshire; Crawley in Sussex; and Harlow and Basildon in Essex. Six other new towns were built in other parts of the country: Corby in Northamptonshire; Cwmbran in Monmouthshire; Peterlee and Newton Aycliffe in Durham; East Kilbride in Lanarkshire; and Glenrothes in Fife. Una Daniels was amongst the first wave to move to Stevenage new town when her husband got a job there in 1951. 'We had been living in a one-bed flat in a shared house in Hendon with our daughter. The landlady was terrible, she only allowed us to hang out washing on a Monday, we had to be in bed by 10 p.m. and if we talked after then, she'd bang on the ceiling. My husband got a job as a safety officer in Stevenage in March '51. When he came back with the keys to the new house, he came bounding up the stairs, picked me up and danced me around the room shouting, "We've got it, we've got it!" I couldn't get to Stevenage quick enough. I went down to the landlady and said, "Mrs Brown, it is our pleasure to say goodbye to you." It was like getting our own little palace. We were never allowed to make any noise in the old place so for the first couple of weeks my daughter went dizzy catching up on all the noise.'

The new town development corporations that built and administered the new towns hoped that the people moving out would enjoy the benefits of both urban and rural life. There was a vision of a new social harmony between all classes of society. As the chairman of the Stevenage Development

During the post-war years there was a great housing drive and the building of millions of new homes, most of them on council or private estates.

New towns and council estates in the countryside offered much-improved housing for those moving out from the cities.

Corporation put it: 'We want to revive the social structure which existed in the old English villages, where the rich lived next door to the not so rich and everyone knew everybody.' It was a curious mixture of utopian socialism and paternalistic conservatism. But from the beginning there were problems. The new towns took much longer to build than was originally imagined and many did not receive their first residents until the early 1950s. By then the Conservatives were back in power and, with little commitment to the new towns project, they cut the budget. Although house-building continued, there was little money for anything like roads, street lighting, schools, transport and community centres. The first residents in new towns like Stevenage were shocked to find themselves marooned on a gigantic building site, which in the winter months turned into a sea of mud. They had to walk miles to the nearest shops and schools. As pioneer resident Michael Cotter put it, 'I felt we had been dumped on the side of a hill and left to our own devices.' This lack of basic amenities was one of the key factors in the much publicized 'new town blues' amongst the first generation of newcomers. Some returned home. The majority stayed though, and formed militant and successful tenants' associations that fought for better services. Michael Cotter became one of the leaders of the Stevenage Tenants' Association in the fifties. 'We were determined to make it work,' he says. 'We organized marches, mass meetings down in the town hall, all sorts of demonstrations.'

Once the new towns began to provide basic facilities they became very popular with the families moving out of the cities. The houses, designed by corporation architects, were usually semi-detached or built in short terraces.

Most had big picture windows and were open-plan. A variety of styles was used and architects tried to make the most of the semi-rural settings. The newcomers loved the privacy and convenience of having the whole house to themselves – it was like heaven after enduring city life in overcrowded rented accommodation. Gina Spreckley moved from north London to Hemel Hempstead in 1957. 'The town had been going for about four years and it was so lovely, it was a completely new life. The house was delightful, I thought this looks just like an illustration out of a magazine. It had a separate dining room and lounge, my daughters had their own bedrooms, we had a modern bathroom with hot running water, a lovely kitchen all to ourselves. And when you looked out of the windows it was all green trees and sunshine, and from the back we could see over fields. After what we'd been through it was such a relief, it was like shedding an old overcoat. From that moment on my daughter's asthma started to get better.'

The GOOD LIFE

Most homes were modern, fitted up for gas and electricity. As well as all the benefits of the latest technology, residents had a garden, front and back, often for the first time, and gardening clubs and horticultural associations blossomed as many working men discovered a new hobby. Life was so good that many of the families settling in the new towns decided to have more children, which led to a higher than average birth rate. David Ritchie, a teacher, managed to get a house in Glenrothes new town in Fife in the late fifties. 'It was fairyland, a new house, with a hedge round the front and a garden and fence round the back, it was marvellous. I'd never had a garden before but now I started growing vegetables, cabbages, turnips. I put raspberry bushes around the fence, we were eating a lot of our own fresh produce. It was a wonderful place to bring up children, with all the greenery and countryside around you. And I remember that at that time there was almost twice as many children born in Glenrothes as the national average in Scotland, which was about two for each family. In Glenrothes then it was four. We had four, our next-door neighbour had three, and five the other side. It was known as nappy valley. We loved the children, they were our life.'

Glenrothes was more successful than most new towns in creating a genuinely mixed community. 'I had a miner on one side, a journalist on another, workers and professional people all lived cheek by jowl. It was very exciting and it strengthened the community.' However, despite the success

A housewife sweeps her path in the newly-rebuilt Gorbals estate in Glasgow. Tenements in this area had been amongst the worst slums in Britain. Redevelopment began in the late fifties.

of the new towns in providing better homes they never achieved their aim of creating genuinely mixed, classless communities. They were highly selective about who they housed. They wanted to promote their image as magnets of success and prosperity, attracting the right kind of people to work on their industrial estates. As a result they siphoned off just one type of person – the skilled worker and his family – not a cross-section of society as had originally been planned. And in most new towns there was very little mixing between the professional and managerial classes and the manual working classes. They generally kept to their own housing developments and estates, with those who could afford higher rents colonizing the better areas.

With the new towns only able to accommodate relatively small numbers of people, the housing shortage in the cities remained. In the fifties the new Conservative government came up with a different solution. This was to build more new flats in the cities. Party politics was turning into a numbers game and the easiest way to achieve impressive figures was to build higher blocks of flats. The fifties was the decade of long concrete slab blocks, most of them six to twelve storeys high – one of the grandest projects in this style was the Loughborough Road estate in Brixton, built between 1954 and 1957. Investing mainly in these medium-level flats, the government achieved a target of around a quarter of a million new homes a year. Though small, they were generally popular as they offered modern facilities the tenants had never enjoyed before.

OUR VERY OWN *Home*

However, the real growth area in the fifties was private, owner-occupied housing. Just after the war less than a third of all homes were privately owned and the majority of owners were middle class – only the minority of breadwinners who enjoyed secure and well-paid jobs contemplated taking on mortgage repayments. The numbers of private homes were further restricted under the Labour government of 1945 to 1951, which permitted only one home to be built for sale for every four local authority homes built for renting. However, the Conservative governments that were in power between 1951 and 1963 reversed these policies, lifting the old controls and encouraging a 'property owning democracy'. As a result, half the new homes built during this period were owner-occupied. In the affluent fifties the ideal of home-ownership started to replace the socialist dream of mass housing planned for the public good by a benevolent state. For the young generation of middle-class newly-weds, buying a home together was an important part of the romantic ideal of married life.

Pamela Woodland was a young teacher from Rotherham. 'I'd been going out with Roland for a year when we decided to get married. We didn't want to live with his mother and I certainly didn't want to live with my parents. It had to be our own home. We decided to marry in the August and we were saving up and we found a house that was £1600. We got a mortgage and they loaned us £1100, but where were we to find the other £500 from? Roland was earning £36 a month and I was earning £27. Now Roland had a beloved motorbike, it was his pride and joy. And he didn't say anything but a few days later he gave me a large envelope. I opened it and it was full of pound notes. I said, "What's this?" And he said, "It's the bike, I've sold it." And that was the first bond between Roland and me. The first act of sacrifice one for the other. From that moment on I knew Roland was the one for me and our marriage has survived forty-eight years.'

By the early sixties increasing numbers of working-class couples were also buying homes of their own. They were often the first in their family to take the plunge into ownership. Irene Ranahan had been engaged to Roger for five years before they married. 'While we waited all that time to get married, we were saving up and hoping that one day we might be able to buy a house of our own. It was a dream really, most of my friends were in rooms in their parents' houses and I thought I can't ever see this coming off. One day I was up at Roger's mother's and Rog came in and said, "I've got a nice surprise for you, we're going to buy our own house". I couldn't believe him, I thought he was joking. "No, no," he said, "come with me." Anyway I went down and it was just a field, and he said, "Well, this is where we're going to live." He'd heard that a builder had bought the land and was going to build some houses. "The man's coming round tonight with the plans and then you can pick the house you want to live in." Well I couldn't believe it, I mean, me, choosing my own house. Well I couldn't wait to tell the girls in the office, and I said, "You'll never believe what my fiancé has done for me, he's going to buy me a house, we're going to have a house of our own." They were all delighted for me, and then I started a trend because all the rest of the girls that were engaged to be married in that office, they all started to look around for their own houses. We went to the building society and they had to work out whether we could afford to pay the mortgage and all the bills that's involved in buying property. And it turned out we could. Well you can imagine, I was that excited about having this house. I couldn't wait to get the camera out because I wanted to savour every moment of the house going up. I felt like a millionaire because now we were starting another life. I was leaving my own family behind and thinking of my future, making ourselves a new life, doing something totally different and exciting.'

Commuter VILLAGES

The majority of home-owning families chose to live away from the cities. The coming of mass car-ownership which began in the fifties brought greater mobility and most people used this to get away from smoky, congested urban areas. They set up home on private estates in the outer suburbs that were developing fast in the fifties and sixties. But increasing numbers of middle-class home-owners wanted to live even further afield, in the countryside. Again, the key factor was the car. Now it was relatively easy to commute directly from a remote village to an office job in the town or city many miles away. The real long-distance travellers usually combined a car and train journey, and often parked at stations.

Many home-owning families chose to get away from the cities and live closer to the countryside. The fifties and sixties saw the rise of the long-distance middle-class commuter.

Many small market towns and villages were ripe for new development as a result of mechanization on farms and locals leaving the land to look for jobs in the cities. Rural Surrey was the first region to be colonized by London commuters. They turned run-down farming communities into metropolitan villages, a trend that spread rapidly throughout the Home Counties, where semi-rural areas became known as the `gin and Jag' belt. Home-owners later began to move to more outlying areas. The electrification of Eastern Region lines to Liverpool Street station opened up many Essex villages to commuters into London in the late 1950s. Over the next decade a similar pattern emerged around most major towns and cities all over Britain. Pretty villages in counties like Oxfordshire, Gloucestershire, Wiltshire, Yorkshire and Suffolk became home-owning, commuter outposts. New housing developments, with custom-built detached homes, some in mock Georgian style, sprouted on the outskirts of villages. The houses often had double garages for the two cars that families needed as a result of long-distance commuting. However, most of the newcomers wanted to buy houses with character and with history. Gentrifiers snapped up period properties at bargain prices of just a few thousand pounds. Then they set about lovingly restoring them. In so doing they gave new life and beauty to rural housing, which had been in serious decline for much of the century.

Rural BLUES

The pioneer middle-class home-owners who moved out of urban areas had high hopes. Escaping from the traffic-choked inner cities and the safe conformity of the suburbs, they were embarking on a great adventure. But their enthusiasm was sometimes dampened as they became aware of the inconveniences and sacrifices of life in the countryside at this time. In the 1950s and early 1960s many villages were poorly served by mains services such as gas, electricity, water and sewers. Many families had to make do with a smelly cesspit in the back garden. Improvements took years and proved costly. To make matters worse, some of the newcomers were viewed with suspicion or shunned by the locals. Those who moved out of cities often shared a romantic ideal that they would be joining a friendly community of rustic villagers. The reality was that local people frequently resented this colonization by townies with posh voices, who were pushing up property prices so much that their own families couldn't afford to live near them any more.

Some young mothers who moved out to isolated hamlets and villages with their commuter husbands were soon dispirited and demoralized. Nan Wise and her husband – a lecturer at Leeds University – bought a cottage in the East Riding village of East Acklam in 1952. 'I was following my husband's dream of a cottage in the country. He loved the cottage, it was very pretty, we had roses round the door. He played for the village cricket team and helped with the harvest. But he was hardly ever there, he was away for days at a time in Leeds. I was by myself with the babies and I was totally isolated. I had no car, there was only one bus a day, there was just a phone box at the top of the hill to communicate with the outside world, and there was nobody like me living there. I was a young middle-class woman with new ideas. I was completely different to everyone else. The East Riding was so remote then, it was like going back a century. There was no electricity, no hot running water in the houses, no inside toilets and they were proud, they didn't want to change. They thought we were mad living there. And I nearly did go mad. I started muttering to myself and I was so lonely. I cried a lot. I was terribly depressed. My husband got me to see a psychiatrist. And I saw the village doctor. He said the reason was that we'd moved to the back of beyond. In the end, after a few years we moved back to the city, I couldn't stand it any more.'

Some of the pioneers who moved into more remote villages had to cope with a lack of basic facilities like gas, electricity and hot running water.

IDEAL HOME

May, 1952   Two Shillings

New Homes Number

New CITY DWELLERS

The growing numbers of aspirational families who were moving away from the cities were replaced by an influx of newcomers, most of them from the New Commonwealth. During the fifties and early sixties there was a large increase in immigration to Britain. Arrivals from the West Indies soared from 1000 in 1952 to 66,000 in 1961 and those from India and Pakistan showed similar increases, with

48,000 arriving in 1961. The key factor that attracted immigrants was the post-war boom in production. It created an acute labour shortage, with Britons reluctant to take dirty, low-paid jobs that involved a lot of shift work. Public transport and hospitals were seriously affected and Britain looked to the New Commonwealth for a reserve army of labour. Some were employed directly from their home countries – in 1956 London Transport began recruiting staff from the Caribbean. And health minister Enoch Powell was involved in the campaign to employ thousands of West Indian women as nurses in the nation's hospitals. Others came unaided as voluntary immigrants. Most had been taught that Britain was their mother country and that they were coming to the promised land. The reality was that they faced much racial prejudice which would hit them hard when it came to finding homes to live in.

A mother and daughter pictured in a dilapidated home in 1950. The new post-war immigrants had to accept squalid and overcrowded rented accommodation in the inner cities.

Many immigrants first looked for cheap rented accommodation which was concentrated in the inner cities. But they met a strong colour bar. Signs stating 'No Coloureds' and 'Europeans Only' appeared in boarding-house windows. The same message was spelt out in 'accommodation available' advertisements in newspapers. White landlords and landladies said they were fearful that taking in 'coloureds' might lower the tone of an area even more and lead to a fall-off in trade. In order to get lodgings, immigrants often had to pay high rents and accept squalid, overcrowded conditions. One landlord who dominated this market in London, and made a fortune, was Peter Rachman. He had arrived in Britain in 1946, a penniless and stateless refugee, having survived a German concentration camp in his native Poland. He moved into the property business and bought around 150 decaying houses in central London. His strategy was to remove the white tenants – sometimes terrorizing them with Alsatian dogs – and pack in as many West Indian immigrants as possible. He soon built up a huge empire of seedy and crumbling properties, most of them in the then unfashionable Notting Hill area.

One of Rachman's tenants was George Rhoden, who arrived from Jamaica in 1961 at the age of twenty. 'I rented a small room from him, me and another guy, there were two beds, one each. We slept at night, then in the daytime two others slept in our beds. So there were four men living there altogether. It was filthy, it was smelly, it was freezing cold in the winter and all we had for curtains was an old blanket. As there was someone sleeping there both night and day it was never opened, it was always dark. We complained but nothing was done. And if you fell behind on the rent, men would come round with dogs to frighten you. We were terrified of the dogs. The worst thing was the rats, there were so many rats. I always thought he was called Ratman because of that. I didn't know his real name was Rachman.'

Some were able to avoid the demoralizing effects of this discrimination and exploitation through home-ownership. By the mid- to late fifties some of the first settlers had saved up enough money to buy cheap houses. In run-down central city areas like Camden and Brixton in London there was a large stock of sub-standard housing that cost very little. The houses were often large and, although they enjoyed few basic facilities, they could accommodate twenty or more people desperate for a temporary home. Chain migration of relatives and friends, often from the same village or town, followed. The availability of cheap and friendly digs in homes owned by West Indians turned Brixton into a reception area for Jamaicans in London, just as Southall became the main centre for immigrants from the Punjab area of India.

The great liberal hope of the fifties and early sixties was that the New Commonwealth immigrants would be assimilated into the British way of life and live next door to white families. The reality was that colour prejudice, chain migration and ethnic pride pushed them into their own separate communities in the cities. Colonies from all over the world re-formed themselves in cities like London, Wolverhampton, Bradford and Bristol. People who shared the same nationality, religion, language and family ties wanted to live close together. There was a flowering of ethnic communities, bringing a new atmosphere and culture to homes and streets in inner-city areas. During the sixties a few of the prosperous ethnic families did move out to suburban homes where there was much more social mixing: the outward migration of Caribbean families from Brixton to Croydon in south London was a well-trodden path. But the original communities remained strong – so strong that they seriously threatened the white residents who lived within them. Many felt swamped by what they regarded as an alien culture and resented the competition for housing that they now faced. This led to further racial tension, which occasionally exploded into race riots like those in 1958 in Notting Hill and Nottingham.

Inner City SLUMS

The housing problems of the inner cities became one of the big issues of the mid- to late sixties. It was not only immigrant families who had to cope with the horrors of appalling accommodation. The outward movement of the more affluent to the suburbs, the new towns and beyond had left behind an excess of people who were semi-skilled, unskilled, old, sick and poor, and who were forced to live in slum conditions that were positively Dickensian. According to some official estimates, in the mid-sixties there were still more than a million city homes that were unfit for human habitation and a further three million lacked basic facilities like hot running water and bathrooms. Amongst the families living in these conditions were many young couples with small children, and single parents.

The Gorbals in 1963. High-rise tower blocks were the sixties solution to the housing crisis in the inner city.

OUT *on the* STREETS

Ironically there was a big demand for cheap rooms, squalid though they often were, as councils were often unable to provide an alternative. Starved of funds, their waiting lists were longer than ever before. Some authorities closed them altogether and, as a result, homelessness – which had gone down in the fifties and early sixties – was on the increase again. In 1966 Ken Loach's drama documentary *Cathy Come Home*, featuring the plight of a homeless woman and her children, was hugely influential in raising awareness of the problem of homelessness. Cassie McConachy was one of the many real-life Cathies who ended up living on the streets of London in the late sixties. 'I was a teenage mum, I got married too young. We lived in rooms and it all went wrong, he was violent to me, so I left him. He didn't give me any money and I didn't have any. My parents didn't want to help me so I had nowhere to go. I had a boy in nappies and I was pregnant and I just stuffed everything in the pram and took off. I was just walking and walking with nowhere to go and you go into zombie mode for a while. I saw everybody going home to their homes and flats to have their tea and I felt so angry and so rejected. I tried to get a room, I went to several places, but when they saw me with a baby and looking like I had no money they didn't want to know. It was hard at the best of times getting a place when you had a baby. So I ended up on King's Cross station and I slept there for a week. I was regularly kicked out and I'd just walk around pushing the baby. My biggest fear was having my son taken into care away from me. In the second week a kind policeman let me sleep in the waiting room and brought me sandwiches and a flask of coffee every night. And he paid for me to stay in a bed and breakfast place and told me about a hostel for the homeless. I was so grateful to him. Mind you, the hostel was hell, they treated you like a prisoner, you were totally institutionalized, but at least I was off the streets.'

THE HIGH RISE *Dream*

With the Labour government back in power between 1964 and 1969 there was a new determination to banish poverty from the Victorian housing ghettos for ever. A short-term radical solution was needed. Politicians, planners and architects all agreed that building high-rise flats was the best way to provide housing that was cheap, quick and attractive. The heart of this new vision of the city beautiful was the system-built tower block. The idea was to stand the street on its end, pointing up to the sky, to save space. The tall slim buildings, some of them twenty-four storeys high, were to be made in factories then erected on site, thus saving time and money. In 1965 the Labour government provided generous grants to fund many slum-clearance and high-rise building programmes. The Victorian slums of Bristol, Birmingham, Bradford, Manchester, Sheffield, Salford and a host of other cities were bulldozed to make way for the tower blocks of the future. London was in the lead, achieving record levels of rehousing through these buildings. Four hundred sprouted in the late sixties. They were opened with municipal splendour, and many won prizes for their design and architecture.

High-rise flats in Gosport, Hampshire. The high-rise dream of modern living in the city quickly turned sour.

To begin with the plan worked. The first residents loved the flats, in particular their spacious interiors and the fact that each one contained a modern kitchen, bathroom and toilet. Many people were excited by the idea of high-rise living and some of the most coveted flats were those on the top floors. They were quieter, the air was more bracing and they enjoyed spectacular views. Hilda White moved to the twelfth floor of a high-rise block in Salford. 'All our street went together to this tower. We were sad to leave our old homes and see them knocked down, but this was real luxury now, a lot better. We had hot water, I was amazed that I could have a hot bath whenever I wanted. And the views, that was the icing on the cake, spectacular views and all down below there were, like, toy cars.' Irene Ranahan used to visit her grandmother who had moved into a tower block in Bristol. 'She loved it there. I remember she said to me, "At least when I die, there won't be so far to get to heaven."'

But the high-rise dream very quickly went wrong as two serious grievances started to turn many tenants against living in tower blocks. First, the lifts were too few, too small and too slow. Worst of all, they were constantly breaking down and could easily be vandalized. Because there was a shortage of money for back-up, they often took a long time to fix and breakdowns meant that those living on the upper levels faced exhausting journeys up and down hundreds of stairs to get in and out of the building. For the old, the sick and mothers with young children the long climbs were an appalling prospect. Some people were stranded for hours or occasionally days at a time. In the late sixties Doreen Reid lived with her husband and baby on one of the top floors of a high-rise block in Plaistow, east London. 'I was virtually stuck in the flat all the time until the lift got going. Sometimes it would take a day, sometimes two days to fix, and I just couldn't get out at all because to take the baby out in the pram was impossible.' The second problem was that the tower blocks were totally unsuited to the needs of families with young children. Lack of play space inside and outside the buildings created a claustrophobic atmosphere. It was impossible to supervise outdoor play and mothers were terrified at the prospect of their children falling off balconies, out of windows or down stairs.

> " "
> THEN ONE MORNING WE HEARD A RUMBLE, I THOUGHT IT WAS A THUNDERSTORM. SUDDENLY MY HUSBAND THREW HIMSELF ON MY HEAD. THEN WHEN I LOOKED UP THE WALL BEHIND OUR BED HAD DISAPPEARED. MY HUSBAND SAID, "GOD, THE FLATS ARE FALLING DOWN."
> " "

What really brought the brief heyday of the tower block to an end was its terrible structural defects. Some of them were inadequately tested and were built to unsafe heights. In 1968 disaster struck. Ronan Point, a brand-new block of system-built flats in east London, partially collapsed and killed five people. Newly-wed Carol Eustace had moved in just six weeks before. 'We were offered number sixty on the twelfth floor and we just fell in love with it. It was so big, so light, it had a wonderful kitchen and bathroom the like of which I'd never seen before. Absolutely gorgeous. We spent all our money getting everything new, new carpets, new furniture, got it really nice. Then one morning we heard a rumble, I thought it was a thunderstorm. Suddenly my husband threw himself on my head. Then when I looked up the wall behind our bed had disappeared. My husband said, "God, the flats are falling down." He opened the lounge door and it fell off and there was just nothing there, the whole of our lounge had gone, we were looking out into the open air. I still had my nightie on but we all managed to clamber down the stairs to safety. We were so lucky to be alive. It was such a shock, but the emotion didn't come out until we had a thunderstorm a few weeks later. I got so upset, it brought it all back. Now every time there is a thunderstorm, that rumble of the thunder brings it all flooding back.'

RENOVATION *and* GENTRIFICATION

A new housing policy came to replace tower blocks: rehab or rehabilitation. Instead of being knocked down, Georgian and Victorian buildings in the inner cities were to be renovated and given a new lease of life. Generous home-improvement grants were offered by the government. The aim was to improve the housing conditions of poorer people and some did indeed benefit. But the main effect was to give a huge impetus to the gentrification of the inner cities by the home-owning professional middle classes.

This had begun in the early 1950s and was most pronounced in London, with Canonbury in the borough of Islington one of the first areas to be gentrified. Some of those who moved into its elegant Georgian town houses were young, bohemian architects like Harley Sherlock. 'We wanted to be in the centre of things, where everybody was, we wanted a change from suburbia which wasn't where life was going on. We wanted to be where working people of all sorts were, and all this we found in Canonbury. In those days properties in central London were cheap, nobody wanted to live in the centre. We bought two very nice buildings, and each house I think cost £2650, which by today's standards is just ridiculous. Most people wanted to live in the leafy suburbs. Indeed my parents thought I was mad to come and live in dirty, grubby old London. But for those of us who were young and wanted to do something different this was an absolutely marvellous opportunity. We were a sort of cooperative of young idealistic architects and we wanted to join the two houses we'd bought together. So we had a sort of housewarming party, we gave the guests pickaxes and crowbars, and we showed them where to make a hole from one house into the other, one at the first floor and one in the basement. And we offered a first prize of a bottle of schnapps for the first person to get through.'

Cleaner air in central city areas helped to promote even more gentrification from the mid-fifties onwards. Until then dreadful smogs had engulfed many cities in the winter months. They reduced visibility to a few inches, they covered everything and everybody with a thin layer of dirt and they caused thousands of deaths by heightening breathing problems, especially amongst the very young and the very old. The Clean Air Acts introduced rigorous smoke controls to most cities in the late fifties and early sixties and brought to an end the era of the 'pea-souper' which had been notorious in London. As cities became cleaner they became viable alternatives to the suburbs for more adventurous middle-class couples who wanted to buy their own homes. The

73

bug-infested buildings that had housed the poor for generations could be bought very cheaply. Another big advantage was their closeness to where most people worked. No longer would it be necessary to spend hours each day commuting in and out of the city. Home-improvement grants were the final incentive that was needed for gentrification take off.

By the late sixties the number of middle-class gentrifiers was increasing rapidly. In London, Islington was the real growth area and, as Canonbury filled up, so the newcomers discovered Barnsbury and set about transforming one of the capital's worst slums into a splendid period suburb. House-hunting young couples became experts at spotting up-and-coming areas. They looked for sand- and cement-mixers on the pavement – telltale signs of restoration – and noted how many houses in a street possessed brass door knockers and were painted white. This was the badge of the pioneer and announced that there was a gentrifier within, determined to restore the house to its former glory.

By the late sixties the colonization of areas like Barnsbury by young professionals had brought a new atmosphere to parts of inner London. Through the newly formed Barnsbury Society the gentrifiers pursued imaginative schemes for tree planting and traffic control which helped to restore the charm of the area's Georgian squares and terraces. The dominant style here – and throughout Britain – was one of elegant austerity or 'conspicuous thrift'. Many of the gentrifiers had been rebellious students and were rejecting the brash materialism and showiness of the affluent society in favour of a natural and unpretentious look. Furniture was stripped pine, walls were painted rather than papered and floorboards were sanded to remove the varnish, then left uncovered. Whilst the gentrifiers wanted all the benefits of modernity like gas, electricity, central heating and washing machines, there was also a huge respect and nostalgia for all things Georgian and Victorian. It was in part a reaction to the huge changes of the previous twenty years, which had seen so much of the nation's old housing destroyed – sometimes mistakenly – in the name of progress.

For most people housing did improve in the 1950s and 1960s. Those who moved out to the new council estates and new towns generally enjoyed homes that were of a much better quality than before. One of the most important factors in this improvement was the spectacular decline of private, rented accommodation, which had once dominated the housing market and was where the worst conditions prevailed. It fell from 60 per cent of all homes at the beginning of the fifties to around 15 per cent by the end of the sixties. Many of the houses once owned by landlords were bought by councils and were demolished and replaced by modern housing. Although serious mistakes were made, the most disastrous being the tower blocks of the late sixties – never again would people trust architects and planners as they had before – many of the medium- and low-rise housing developments were a genuine improvement. Those who gained least – and who suffered most – were the unskilled, the poor, the single parents and the elderly, many of whom were trapped in the worst housing conditions in the inner cities.

The other huge change in the fifties and sixties, one which benefited those involved, was the massive rise in home-ownership. The number of owner-occupiers almost tripled, increasing from just over three million in 1950 to over eight million by the late 1960s. It was a new trend driven by full employment and greater affluence and gave families much greater choice and control over where they lived. They could build extensions, knock down walls, paint exteriors and decorate interiors how they liked. Most important, they could move where they wanted, when they wanted. And rising house prices proved that home-ownership was also a good investment for the future. By the late sixties the old ideals of public housing schemes were fading fast. A home rented from the council was seen as second-class.

Many areas in west London were renovated and gentrified in the sixties.

OMO adds Brightness to whiteness

- adds Brightness to coloureds too!

All Mod Cons

I F THERE WAS ONE SYMBOL OF THE NEW, ALL MOD CONS Britain of the fifties and sixties it was the washing machine. In 1950 it had been a luxury, a privilege enjoyed only by a wealthy few, but mass production, a growing demand and hire purchase ensured that the cost of a washing machine fell steadily over the next twenty years and by the late sixties in most homes one took pride of place in the new gas or electric kitchen. The washing machine helped to usher in a revolution in British home life. In the fifties and sixties, this and other mechanical helping hands came to the rescue of the overworked housewife. For the first time the lady of the house could be liberated from the kitchen sink. No longer was it necessary for her to clean, dust, polish, brush and scrub by hand to keep the house clean. At the end of the sixties the average home contained an array of labour-saving modern appliances, from washing machines to vacuum cleaners, cookers to refrigerators, that would have been pure fantasy twenty years earlier.

Previous page Like many other washing powder brands in the fifties, Omo promised the housewife a whiter, cleaner wash.

> " "
>
> THE FIREPLACE NOT ONLY HEATED YOU, IT BOILED YOUR WATER, IT COOKED YOUR FOOD, IT WAS WHERE YOU HAD YOUR BATH, IT WAS THE MAIN HUB OF THE HOUSE. I REMEMBER MY MUM USED TO PUT MY NIGHTIE IN THE OVEN TO GET ME WARM BEFORE I WENT TO BED.
>
> " "

But back in the early fifties most housework was done by hand and keeping house was as arduous as it was time-consuming. Many women spent over two-thirds of their waking hours cleaning and cooking – no wonder then that most of them felt like slaves to their home and tumbled exhausted into bed at the end of the day. The middle-class housewife could no longer depend on a paid skivvy to assist her. Two world wars and better wages in munitions factories had given women in service a taste of independence, and few chose to return to life as a servant when there was greater freedom and money to be found in jobs in factories, shops and offices. Middle-class women found themselves servantless and were forced to become their own chief cooks and bottle-washers – as most working-class women had always been.

These were the days of domestic drudgery. Most houses ran on a combination of elbow grease and inefficient fuel. Coal fires were the main source of heat but they required constant attention, were dirty and expensive to run. Most families kept the fire going only in the room where they spent most of their time. 'Shut that door' was the common cry whenever anyone left it, taking the warm air with them, and many people awoke in the morning to find frost on the inside of their windows. 'We did everything in one room and that was the room with the fireplace in it,' remembers Jo Jones from north Wales. 'The fireplace not only heated you, it boiled your water, it cooked your food, it was where you had your bath, it was the main hub of the house. I remember my mum used to put my nightie in the oven to get me warm before I went to bed. It was really hard work because we used to have to clean the flue out in the morning, there'd be dust everywhere, and then keep the fire stoked all day, you couldn't let it go out.'

Not only was there dirt and drudgery to contend with inside the home, but the fifties family also endured a constant battle against grime outside it. Most people lived in towns and cities dominated by the manufacturing industry, which used coal as a fuel. For the majority of working-class people, who lived in the terraced streets surrounding factories and mills, life was an endless struggle against filth and pollution. 'Everywhere there was black smoke pouring out of the factory chimneys,' says Eileen Cook from the mill town of Colne in Lancashire, 'plus every house had a fire, so you had rows and rows of houses all with smoke going up the chimneys. It was horrendous, everybody had bad coughs and catarrh, you felt filthy. And in wintertime when we got the thick fogs they smelt as well, it was just like being in a dirty sticky cloud.'

The domestic battle against dirt was important for health reasons – diseases flourished in unclean homes – and was made more difficult by poor housing and a lack of modern facilities. However, as well as the practical needs of hygiene, keeping a house clean was a source of pride and respectability. A woman's standing in society was reflected by the cleanliness of her home, and even if she had little money she would stress that though she was poor, she at least managed to keep her children clean.

Keeping up appearances was a priority. 'My mother had a saying,' remembers Eva Kay from Blackburn. 'It went: "Always keep your front doorstep clean, do your windows and clean your net curtains because more folk will pass by than ever call in."' Eileen Cook felt the pressure to keep up standards of cleanliness in her street. 'I had to be out washing my doorstep every Thursday morning. If you weren't doing it by quarter past nine people thought you must be ill, they'd be knocking on the door asking if you were all right. There were a lot of old women living up my street and they were traditionalists. They'd soon pull you up if you weren't out there first thing, you couldn't have a lie-in. They'd say that we were a respectable street. You'd be out there with your bucket and brush scrubbing and swilling, then you donkey-stoned your step, did your windows, wiped your front door down. Oh, and you'd do your letter box too. It took about an hour and a half to two hours to get it sorted out.' All of that before starting on the inside of the house. The arrival of powered helping hands was eagerly awaited.

Cleanliness is next to Godliness. Cleaning the doorstep and paving outside the home was a weekly ritual for many housewives.

POWER *for the People*

Most middle-class families living in towns and cities had some form of power – gas or electricity – in their homes, but usually only in one or two rooms. Electricity had been installed in a haphazard way since the 1920s but, although post-war statistics in 1946 showed that 86 per cent of households were wired for electricity, this was not done to today's standards. Wiring was often of poor quality and liable to blow circuits, while electric appliances came, confusingly, with three different types of plug and ten types of fuse. It was quite common for people to limit themselves to one or two power points in the home or only install lighting. 'We only had the lights downstairs,' recalls Pat Dallimore from Bristol. 'I'd be petrified of going upstairs at night, I used to beg my dad to leave the light on in the hall so that I could find my way to bed.'

Electricity was the key to the domestic revolution in the fifties.

Many people who lived in rural areas, especially in south-west England, were without electricity throughout the fifties. Their world was a dingy place. 'In the fifties we only had old gaslights, there was a mantle and if you turned it on, held the match too close and broke the mantle, well that was it, you had no light then,' remembers Cornishman John Harris. 'There wasn't much light anyway, so we generally went to bed early. I used to do a bit of reading by candlelight but it was such a strain, it's a wonder my eyes weren't ruined. I suppose we were quite primitive, cooking on a Cornish range, having an open fire and living by candlelight. The radio worked with an accumulator which was like a huge battery, we used to take it to the local radio shop in a pushchair. It would last about a week and towards the end of the week we'd have our ears up to the wireless straining to hear the news. Of course, there was no light in the bathroom, so if you wanted a bath in the evening you had to take a candle up, and if there was too much steam the candle went out. Having candles and gaslight was dingy and dark, it's a wonder we managed to do anything at all.'

The key to the post-war domestic revolution lay in mains electricity supplied by a new network constructed in the fifites, the supergrid. 'The joy of better light, of warmth and the power to make easier work of life's daily chores' according to one advertisement. In fact, electricity has probably done more than any other factor to change lives in Britain since the war. Regulations introduced in 1950 ensured that newly built homes had proper ring mains and standardized sockets, and owners of older houses were encouraged to update their wiring in preparation for the new era. Electricity was to be the lifeblood of the modern home.

However, many rural areas had to wait until the early 1960s to get mains electricity. The 1962 documentary film *Power Comes to Widecombe* shows the inhabitants of the Dartmoor village celebrating the switching on of the current that brought them out of a gloomy, half-lit world. The coming of electricity was treated as a milestone, and the excitement was so great that some people proudly showed off their naked light bulbs. Jo Jones was a teenager growing up in rural Flintshire when electricity arrived in her village. 'We were told it was coming in twelve months' time so we had the whole house wired with these thick grey cables crawling round the rooms, and lived in huge anticipation of the great switch-on. My friends had had it for months before we finally got it. It was fantastic when it arrived, you could have a light on wherever you wanted it. I'd been used to sharing a table with my father in the evening while I did my homework and he did other stuff, but now I could go upstairs and work in my own room. There was a light switch there and we put in an electric fire. It worked out really well because we didn't have that "being on top of one another" feeling any more.' Having electricity expanded the living space in the home. People were no longer confined to one room for heat and light and the whole house was opened up to them.

Electric fires tempted customers with instant heat at the flick of a switch.

81

The AGE *of the* APPLIANCE

As coal shortages eased after the war, Britain's newly nationalized electricity industry began to promote the use of electricity zealously. It was necessary to persuade people to use more units so that the price of power would reduce for industry as well as for homes. In 1953 income tax and purchase tax were slashed in a bid to encourage spending. The age of austerity was at an end; the age of prosperity was about to start. Life at home had meant doing without. Now basic electric appliances were creeping into the shops and a visit to an electricity showroom tempted customers with its display of gleaming new labour-saving devices. At first, though, it was a case of looking but not buying. The war effort had left the country in heavy debt and the government, desperate for money, urged manufacturers into a big export drive with the slogan 'Export or die'. Advertisements carried warnings of long waiting lists. Marguerite Patten, the domestic guru of the era, recalls, 'You couldn't buy refrigerators, you couldn't buy new cookers, new washing

Young housewives dreamt of filling their kitchens with mod cons.

machines, we had to export them because if we didn't export, as a country we would go under. It was a shattering message to give to people, that we had to wait and wait for all the new equipment of the time.'

But once the restrictions were lifted, there was no stopping the boom in electrical goods. For the young housewife with money to spend on equipping her home, the showrooms contained the stuff of dreams – shiny white machines to ease the drudgery of housework. After years of scrimping and saving the general public was unfamiliar with the new appliances on the market so, to encourage people to buy, the showrooms hired demonstrators. Even though it was women who stood to benefit

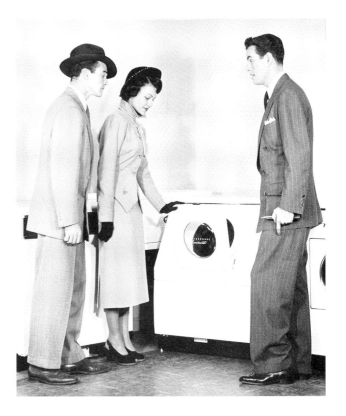

A washing machine was the top appliance on everyone's shopping list.

most from the new mod cons, sexism was rife and the demonstrators focused on men. 'If a woman came in with her husband we would try and attract his attention because we knew that he was going to pay the bill at the end of the day,' remembers Joan Viveash from Somerset, who was a demonstrator from 1958 onwards. 'We would show him how efficiently the machines worked, we went through the economics of it because this was something you had to make appear to the benefit of the husbands. You would try to get a sisterly fellow feeling with the wife, but at the same time you were also being a little seductive to the husband and suggesting that if he was a real man he was going to see that the woman in his life was well looked after. We'd make the point, with a washing machine or a spin dryer for instance, that he would have a much happier lifestyle because he would come home on wash day and, instead of finding a frazzled wife and dripping laundry all round the place, the wife would be feeling content, the meal would be ready which otherwise might not be the case and he would be a happier man. It was a technique that always seemed to work.' Ed Mitchell from Norfolk was convinced. 'When my wife announced she was pregnant for the third time at the age of forty-three, I took her down the showroom and got her a Parnell washing machine. I wanted to save her having to put her hands in that cold water and wash all those children's things again.'

Wash Day BLUES

The automatic washing machine was the most prized mod con of the new electricity age. In 1950 less than 5 per cent of households had a powered one and it was the top appliance on everyone's shopping list. Laundry was the aspect of housework that most enslaved women and Monday was traditionally set aside to do it. Wash day was the most labour-intensive day of the week, and it is not surprising that it came after Sunday – housewives needed a day of rest to brace themselves for the task ahead, which was little altered since their grandmothers' day. A good deep sink, a scrubbing board and lots of hot water were the essentials as, for much of the fifties, many women were still doing the washing by hand. Once the clothes had been rinsed several times they were fed through a mangle to squeeze out the water. There was machinery to help with the load. One example was the wash boiler, powered by gas, electricity or coal, which brought clothes to the boil. However, even such equipment didn't take the labour out of the laundry. 'By the time I'd washed, rinsed, hung out to dry and then ironed, I was ready to drop. The whole day was spent on the washing,' remembers Olive Morgan from south Wales.

One step on the road towards the automatic washing machine was the single- and, later, twin-tub machine to which an electrically powered mangle or wringer was attached. Jo Roffey was a mother living in Kent when she finally got one. 'Because I had six children and no washing machine I did everything by hand, used to boil all the nappies up for the babies and of course it had to be done continuously, you couldn't afford to get behind with it. I didn't just wash every day, some days I was washing all day just to keep up with it all. It was a real palaver. Somebody gave me a spin dryer but I only had it five minutes before it conked out. So I said to my mate, "I don't know what I'm going to do." She said, "Don't muck about with getting another one of them, get yourself a washing machine." I'd never given it a thought up till then, so my husband got me a twin-tub on H.P. And you know what, I don't know how I ever coped without it, it made a huge difference to my life. Now I wasn't stuck with the washing all day, every day. It took us years to pay off but it was worth every penny.' It's no surprise, then, that washing

WASHING POWDERS

Washing powders were becoming more effective, promising the housewife a whiter, cleaner wash, and there were more of them. The first soapless detergents – became available in Britain in 1950. Instead of the traditional fats and alkalis they used complex chemicals, many of which came from mineral oils. Tide arrived from America in the same year 'for the clean, clean, cleanest weekly wash of all!' Surf was launched in 1952, Daz in 1953 and then, in 1954, there was the relaunch of Omo: 'adds brightness to whites and coloureds too!'

machines were a huge hit. By 1969 two-thirds of households had one, with the biggest increase coming between 1955 and 1966 when the figures leapt from 17.5 per cent to 60 per cent. Not only was it top of the shopping list, in some cases it was top of the wedding list. When Ann Brooke of Surrey decided to get married she opted for a washing machine instead of an engagement ring.

Drying clothes and bedlinen had always been a problem, especially in the uncertain British climate. Housewives usually looked for a bright, breezy day to hang their laundry in the garden. However, the challenge wasn't only to pick the right day. There were standards to be maintained even on the washing line. 'If your washing wasn't as white or sparklingly clean as your neighbours, then you were bringing down the tone of the neighbourhood,' recalls Eileen Cook. 'You couldn't just hang out any old thing. We had a private back street which is where I pegged out the washing, and you know you had to be very particular not just how clean your clothes were but make sure they weren't ragged or needed mending. They had to look good on the line because all the world was going to see, so you didn't put anything out if it was patched.'

The hi-tech way to dry clothes was to use a spin dryer. These were even more popular than washing machines in the early days of mod cons. Domestic goddess Marguerite Patten demonstrated the appliance on television. 'The problem was what to do in a modern house with nowhere to hang the clothes on a wet day. People had the airers that they let down from the ceiling but you couldn't do that with dripping wet clothes, so they had to sit there until the sun came out or the wind got up. So the spin dryer really was a wonderful development. It was small and compact, ideal for the post-war kitchen and could fit

Having an automatic washing machine transformed wash day, the most labour-intensive time of the week. It was no longer necessary to spend all day on the washing.

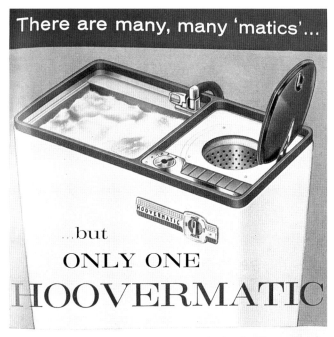

There are many, many 'matics'...

...but

ONLY ONE

HOOVERMATIC

The only 'matic' with exclusive pulsator 'boiling action'

Many to choose from? Yes! First *this-a-matic* then *that-a-matic* . . . and after you've considered the many conflicting claims, you'll probably be very confused. Relax for a moment – the solution is simple. Before you buy *any* washing machine . . . you owe it to yourself to see your Hoover dealer. Ask for a demonstration and then *compare*. Your final choice will be obvious.

Then, to the evidence of your own eyes, there's this further assurance – Hoover quality is accepted as second-to-none by housewives all over the world. Only Hoover 'know-how' gained from years of experience could produce the *Hoovermatic* – with the finest washing system money can buy. How right you'll be to choose the Hoovermatic.

With the Hoovermatic you enjoy all these advantages! ● Exclusive pulsator 'boiling action', the superlative water washing action that gives you the cleanest, quickest, and most thorough wash you have ever seen. ● Twin tubs for twice the speed . . . whilst one tub washes, the other automatically rinses and damp-dries. ● A full family wash in half an hour. ● Automatic timer . . . controls washing time for all fabrics. ● Beautiful and compact design to fit neatly into your kitchen. ● Stainless steel tub . . . cannot rust or chip.

PRICE : **£79.19.5** *(tax paid)* **£85.2.7** *(tax paid — with built-in heater).*

If you judge your wash by cleanness . . . it's got to be HOOVER

into the cupboard under the stairs. They were efficient too, they extracted so much of the water that when you pulled out your man-made fibres, those nylon shirts and the rest, they were virtually ready to go on the hanger and the rest was ready to iron. The spin dryer made a tremendous difference on wash days.'

The alternative to doing your washing at home was to use a launderette. These started to appear on high streets in the late fifties, equipped with the new front-loading automatic washing machines that combined washing and spin-drying. The nation had never washed its dirty linen in public in such a way before, but by the sixties the new 'coin-ops' were becoming the hip places for young people living in flats and bedsits to hang out. 'Coin-ops were brilliant,' remembers Cassie McConachy in west London. 'It was like a party, you'd end up chatting to someone and stay all night.' For Irene Ranahan from Bristol the launderette was the place to go to catch up on neighbourhood news. 'I'd go at lunch time, take my sandwiches and have a chit-chat with people there. The lady would come along and make sure everything was working all right. All the while you'd be talking to the people on either side and gathering a little bit of information about what had been going on. Somebody's moved out, somebody's got married, oh guess what, somebody's had a baby. The launderette was a great way of staying in touch.'

COOK *Electric*

Next to the washing machine, the most popular mod con was the electric cooker. Well into the fifties some households were still struggling with basic cooking utensils like iron kettles and pots that hung from hooks over an open fire; and many were still using old-fashioned coal-fired ranges, although gas gradually replaced solid fuel. An electric cooker with its instant heat was one of the most desirable features of the modern kitchen. 'It was such a novelty to have this mysterious red, glowing thing,' says John Harris. 'Everything got burnt at first, you'd put your hand over the top to see how hot it was and end up burning your fingers on these huge rings glowing red. It was much more powerful than we realized, the saucepans would go on and every now and then mother would end up burning one out. It changed the way we cooked too. With the old Cornish range we'd have a stew on the go most of the time and just add to it. Now we could cook a meal from scratch in minutes.' For housewife Irene Ranahan, having an electric cooker was to be the crowning glory of her modern kitchen. 'For years we'd had to cook on gas. I'd see these

Hollywood films with Rock Hudson and Doris Day in their wonderful American kitchen with all these beautiful things. I'd drift off into a fantasy world thinking "I'd kill for an electric cooker". I was thrilled when they started appearing in our shops. I was one of the first down the showroom for a demonstration.'

A sales battle, which had been brewing between gas and electricity during the inter-war years, intensified in the new era of affluence. Each had their own showrooms in towns and cities, and even in the countryside there was no escape – the electricity and gas boards treated housewives to travelling showrooms. Each also had its own domestic goddess touring the country. While Marguerite Patten demonstrated the joys of cooking electric, another television cook, Fanny Cradock, was doing the same for gas. According to Marguerite, 'People were unsure about cooking electric initially because it was new to them. They thought it

Clever you !

It's a G.E.C. cooker

This is the 'Supreme' – to-day's most exciting cooker, with automatic timing and every up-to-date device.

The king-size eye-level grill has six grilling positions and is almost a cooker in itself. The hob, served by either 3 or 4 Superspeed plates with simmer control, gives you fast, *flexible, see-able* heat. The 36 lb-turkey-size oven has an inner glass door and a removable roof for easy cleaning. You can warm dishes for a big dinner party in the separately-heated storage drawer. Castors make the cooker easily movable. In white or honeysuckle, with green, red or blue switch panel. 3-plate 'Supreme' £74, 4-plate £79,

complete with 150-page cookery book to inspire you !

That's the best of choosing a cooker made by big people like the G.E.C. Extra good design and absolute efficiency come naturally to a firm which is helping both housewives and industry to enjoy more and more benefits from electricity.

See the 'Supreme' and other beautiful G.E.C. *cookers at your electrical suppliers,* and write to the Domestic Equipment Group of The General Electric Co Ltd,Magnet House, Kingsway, London, WC2, for 'Living Electrically with G.E.C.', a handbook of appliances that make life wonderful.

132

was slow to boil and simmer on the hob, even though it was quick in the oven. The one question I was always being asked was "Is it economical?" People were very cost conscious and knew a bit about watts and volts and how much the cookers used. Sometimes people would query the size of the oven, because they thought it looked small. I'd respond by demonstrating that you could cook a 20-pound turkey in it. It always amused me, because when would people ever get to cook a 20-pound turkey?'

Irene Ranahan was one of those who attended Marguerite's showroom demonstrations to pick up tips on cooking electric. 'I was a bit nervous at first, I'd put the pan on one twirly ring and end up switching the wrong ring on and I was forever burning my hand on the hot hob. But if something boiled over, you could clear it up straightaway. It was very modern, clean and fast. And they started making electric cookers in different colours. I got one in chocolate brown which looked a dream in my cream-coloured kitchen. It was a Tricity Marquise, so beautiful, all chrome. Eventually I put it on one day and the sides blew out, so I bought another one, even more sophisticated with a grill inside the oven.'

> Having an electric cooker was the crowning glory of many fifties kitchens.

CHILLING *Out*

When it came to refrigerators, the British public needed more persuasion. People would ask, 'Why on earth do we need a fridge in our climate?' Food was usually kept in a larder or pantry on the cool north or east side of the kitchen, with stone floors and shelves to keep the temperature down. Meat was covered with a wire mesh to keep the flies off. Keeping perishables for any length of time was impossible and housewives who lived in towns were forced to shop almost daily.

> ❝
>
> WHEN I GOT ONE,
> [A REFRIGERATOR] IT WAS
> ABSOLUTELY MINUTE, BUT I WAS
> THRILLED BECAUSE I WAS ABLE TO
> PUT FOOD IN AND NOT HAVE THAT
> AWFUL GREEN FUR – DAMP
> MILDEWY STUFF THAT HAPPENED
> AFTER A DAY OR TWO
> IN A PANTRY.
>
> ❞

It was the glamour of 1950s America that helped to convince Britons of the joys of refrigeration. Over there, ice was something that was added to drinks like Coca-Cola while in Britain it was something to be tolerated on the windows in winter. Hollywood played a role in persuading women that the refrigerator was an essential in the dream kitchen. It wasn't just good for hygiene, it was a style icon too. For Pat Dallimore and her mother it was a trip to the movies that finally persuaded them to take the plunge. 'One film we saw had these poor people living in the Midwest. They were supposed to be poor and yet the mother opened up this great big fridge, took out a big bottle of milk, filled a glass up and gave it to her little boy. But he left it on the table after just a sip. Sitting in the cinema I was gobsmacked. How could he do that, how could he leave a whole glass of milk? We were only having half a glass of milk and half of water and I thought he was supposed to be poor. We came to the conclusion that America must be a wonderland because this woman was poor and yet she had a great, big fridge. Well, the prime minister was going on about how "you never had it so good". He said go out and have it all on H.P., so that's exactly what our ma did. And while others up our way were getting vacuum cleaners, our ma's ambition was to get a fridge, just like in the film.' Refrigerators had a ring of magic about them. Cynthia Hammond from Bournemouth was captivated. 'I couldn't quite believe that I'd actually got one. We used to creep down at night and listen to this wondrous thing working.'

Most of the early refrigerators in Britain were much smaller than American ones – the USA was twenty years ahead of Britain in domestic appliances – but the fridge still won its place in the home. 'When I got one, it was absolutely minute,' remembers Christine Fagg from Hertfordshire, 'but I was thrilled because I was able to put food in and not have that awful green fur – damp mildewy stuff that happened after a day or two in a pantry.' In 1956 only 8 per cent of homes had a refrigerator, but by 1969 this had leapt to 65 per cent. The fridge changed the way we shopped. Its ability to keep food fresh meant that women no longer had to make that daily trip to the shops, and when fridge-freezers came along in the late sixties it was possible to preserve food for even longer periods.

Kitchen QUEEN

The fifties were a time of fashionable domesticity and the kitchen was the heartland of family life. Men were enjoying home comforts after the rigours and deprivation of the war and women were happy to make sure they had them. For the housewife the kitchen was not only her workroom; it also served as restaurant, laundry and nursery rolled into one. While the appliances themselves were getting an upgrade, attention focused on the kitchen itself. Using time-and-motion studies scientists suggested new designs that would bring together all the appliances and save the housewife moving unnecessarily between the separate units. The result was the fitted kitchen and it became the ultimate status symbol of the modern home, its ranks of

In the sixties more and more gadgets started to arrive on the kitchen worktops.

glossy cupboards keeping everything neatly out of sight and cleaning to a minimum. Christine Fagg got hers in the early fifties. 'As we were building a new house, we decided that we would create a kitchen where everything fitted perfectly, which was unheard of at that time because you just had a cooker in the middle of one wall and a sink in the middle of another. And so we worked out inch by inch how we could fit the fridge in, how we could fit the cupboards, where we could put our brooms and stuff. When the fitter came to put in the gas cooker, he was amazed. "My word," he said, "what a stroke of luck, this is going to fit exactly into the space." But of course it was nothing to do with luck, we had worked it out in detail. He'd just never seen a fitted kitchen before. Towards the end of the fitting the boss of the local gas company came up to oversee it and he said, "I can assure you, Mrs Fagg, there's not another kitchen in town to touch it. It will be a showplace for all your friends and neighbours." I was bursting with pride.'

With the fitted kitchen came even more gadgets. The worktops in the sixties kitchen flaunted technology in the form of electric mixers, liquidizers, electric kettles and toasters. The world's first automatic electric kettle, the K1, had gone on sale in 1955. One of the most versatile appliances of the era, the Kenwood Chef, was launched at the 1950 Ideal Home Exhibition. The ambition of its designer, Kenneth Wood, was to make products that would start out as luxuries and become essentials in the home. His first creation was a toaster, followed by a twin-beater mixer before he came up with the classic Kenwood Chef. Advertisements of the time suggested that by using such modern gadgets the housewife could be glamorous despite the domestic demands made on her. All she had to do was whisk off her frilly apron when her husband returned from work, and greet him with a home-made cake rustled up in no time in a food mixer.

Some women were overwhelmed by the technological sophistication of their new kitchen equipment. Gina Spreckley, a Hertfordshire housewife, was given a pressure cooker. 'My husband was a great one for gadgets but I hated them. Well one day he went to the Ideal Home Exhibition and to my astonishment, because he was quite tight, he gave me this gigantic pressure cooker, it was one of the first pressure cookers to come out. So I dutifully got the recipe book and thought we'd have stuffed breast of lamb, cauliflower, new potatoes, stewed gooseberries and rice

The Kenwood Chef had pride of place in many kitchens.

pudding for supper. Now I wasn't used to pressure cookers and I didn't realize that they took about twenty minutes to cool down before you could take the lid off. Everybody was moaning about supper being late, I really should have started cooking the meal twenty minutes earlier than I did. So I approached the pressure cooker with a carving fork and prodded the valve which spun round and suddenly a stream of mutton fat and cauliflower exploded all over the kitchen and down the walls. I looked inside and the stuffed breast of lamb was smothered in gooseberry pips, I had to wash it under warm water. We managed a dinner of sorts from the remains, but I never used that cooker again. It was one kitchen gadget too far.'

Although the mod cons of the fifties and early sixties lightened the burden of housework consid-erably, women soon discovered that the visions of a life of leisure shown in advertisements were still outside their reach. In fact, the appliance of science led to more being expected of them – clothes had to be whiter, the home had to be cleaner, the meals better. A Mass Observation survey in 1957 showed that the jobs undertaken by a typical housewife started at 7.30 in the morning and went on until 10.30 at night. However, most women were proud of being queen of the domestic scene – they had been raised to expect their main role in life to be to provide lovingly for their husband and children. 'What you had to do was get your man, get married, have babies and look after a house, that's what we were brought up to do,' says Pat Mancini in Manchester. 'Well I tried to be a perfect housewife. I did try my very best, I kept it clean and I put good food on the table.'

Now that the middle-class wife was doing her own housework it took a jump in status. No longer was it something done by mere skivvies; it was elevated to the rank of a domestic science. Women were encouraged to be professional in their approach. Pamela Woodland of Rotherham had a job as a teacher, but was still determined to be a domestic goddess. 'I was mistress in my kitchen and that is how I liked it. I did everything. I knew where everything was. My kitchen was like a very, very efficient workshop. Roland, my husband, never came into the kitchen, so I did all the cooking, all the preparation, all the washing up. He didn't know the first thing about the washing machine, he didn't know the first thing about ironing, and he didn't

Hey **Presto**
the secret of perfect pressure cooking

Invest in a Presto for perfectly cooked meals and *lower fuel bills*. You'll be amazed at the speed with which it cooks. You'll be thrilled at the flavour of the food because Presto cooking seals in all the original goodness. The Presto Pressure Cooker is the easiest to use because you see at a glance when pressure is correct. Why not get your Presto today? It will soon pay for itself by the enormous amount of fuel it saves. Popular model 77/6. Large 105/- or with special deep lid 111/-. Separator sets 7/6 and 8/6.

Presto Pressure Cookers conform to the require-ments of the British Standards Institution.

ONLY THE PRESTO

has this one-piece auto-matic pressure device. Watch the silver bands appear : 1 band for fruit bottling ; 2 bands for vegetable bottling ; 3 bands showing for day-to-day cooking.

Presto PRESSURE COOKER **saves ¾ cooking time**

NATIONAL PRESSURE COOKER CO. (England) LTD. Fort Works, Wolverhampton

The pressure cooker was a kitchen gadget too far for Gina Spreckley.

Lucky Girl!

she's got *Sky-line* 'CHEF' CUTLERY

-it's hollow-ground

'Sky-line' new Chef hollow-ground cutlery is getting a warm welcome from housewives for it's really good looking, utterly practical in the kitchen . . . and is so reasonably priced. Such a variety of knives meet every cutting need, with Sheffield stainless steel blades hollow-ground for lasting sharpness and smart rosewood handles to give you a comfortable grip. Attractively boxed, these modern aids in the home make wonderful gifts too. You can also choose individual knives from the self-service 'Sky-line' display at your dealers.

These are the popular 'Chef' sets by 'Sky-line'

4005 5-piece set as illustrated above (Paring, Utility, French Cook's, Carving and Bread Knives) ... Price 30/-

4032 2-piece carving set (Carving Knife and Fork) ... Price 15/6

4026 3-piece carving set (Carving Knife, Fork and Steel) ... Price 25/-

4043 3-piece boxed set (Carver, Bread and French Cook's Knives) ... Price 21/6

4033 Carded set (Cook's, Utility and Paring Knives) ... Price 10/11

Also obtainable as single pieces from 2/11 at your favourite store or ironmonger.

Hightime you had Sky-line   *they start sharp—stay sharp*

By the makers of (**Prestige**) housewares

92

know the first thing about the cooker. It was my ambition to run the house to the best of my ability. Being a housewife was a twenty-four-hour job so I allotted myself an additional two evenings a week to my home.

However, with the sexual revolution of the sixties the idea that being a perfect housewife was an end in itself began to lose credibility and maintaining high standards of housework became oppressive. The seeds of discontent were sown and women started to look beyond the home for a sense of fulfilment. 'I was fighting like mad to get out of the bloody kitchen,' says Vivien Allen from the Isle of Man. 'There was all this propaganda about nest-building and a woman's place being in the home. I felt domestic life was perfectly terrible, I nearly went mad with it. It's soul-destroying spending all day alone cleaning and only having conversations with people aged under six.' Younger women, in particular, were no longer content to be captives in their homes.

In Britain the first generation to enjoy household technology en masse was also the first to have benefited from an extended secondary education. Many of these women felt they had good brains going to rust and having the mod cons enabled them to escape the bondage of the home and spread their wings a little. The automated appliances saved time and effort and enabled women to turn their attention away from housework to other things, be it further education, a job or simply more of a life outside the home. In Christine Fagg's case, mod cons had a major impact on her life. 'My trouble was that I wanted desperately to do things outside my home and all the time I was reaching out and struggling to educate myself further. I was always trying to think of short cuts to the housework, to get out and stimulate my own interests, and that's where the washing machine, the Hoover, etc really came into their own. As the years rolled by and the children were growing up, I had no career, no qualifications and so I knew I must prepare for something. At this time they had just started to run courses for adults at colleges of further education. This was another huge step forward because throughout the war there had been no such thing, so wives couldn't do anything if they hadn't got the qualifications before they married. I signed on for various courses, which in turn put me on course for a rewarding career.'

Mod cons played a supporting role in the emergence of women's liberation in the sixties, which in turn led to an exodus of women out of the home and into the work place. In 1951 one in five women worked outside the home. By the end of the decade this had risen to one in three, and by the late sixties working women had become the norm. What had started as a means of helping women around the home ultimately became a way of facilitating their escape.

The fifties idea of the domestic goddess went out of fashion with the sexual liberation of the sixties.

Food *and* Drink

THE FIFTIES WAS THE FIRST DECADE OF THE celebrity chef. There was even a celebrity chef couple: Fanny and Johnnie Cradock. Together they rode the crest of culinary success. In showbiz style they topped the bill at the Royal Albert Hall. Their television series, which began in 1953, encouraged women to aspire to gourmet levels of cuisine and elegant dining style. Fanny appeared in evening gowns and fur while the monocled Johnnie hovered attentively in a dinner jacket, and together they attempted to demystify the art of cordon bleu cooking and educated the British public about wine. As a child Fanny had spent winters in Nice, where she would sneak into the hotel kitchen and watch the chefs at work. She revered French cuisine, regarding it as the height of the sophistication she sought to pass on to her viewers. Few tried her recipes in the fifties – they were too impractical – but her popularity encapsulated something of the British aspiration towards better eating and drinking.

Previous page Fanny Cradock was one of the first celebrity chefs.

Most people had been forced to endure nearly fifteen years of rationing, which had dulled the appetite, and families had learnt to stretch a little very far. They had endured long queues at shops and had turned to their vegetable patches to provide them with food. Now they wanted a better quality of life and better food. This is the story of how, for most of them, that wish was fulfilled. The fifties and the sixties brought food in abundance and greater culinary diversity to the nation. Cookery became a social skill. Shopping was revolutionized. There was a boom in convenience foods. And the basic British 'meat and two veg' was eclipsed by a taste for all manner of exotic dishes, some from abroad and some the result of scientific developments.

A wearied Britain endured food rationing until 1954, longer than any other western nation including the vanquished Germany. In the post-war years rations actually fell well below the wartime average – the standard allowance each week for a man was just 13 ounces of meat, $1\frac{1}{2}$ ounces of cheese, 6 ounces of butter and margarine, 1 ounce of cooking fat, 8 ounces of sugar, 2 pints of milk and a single egg. Spam, the wartime substitute for decent meat, remained ubiquitous and even horsemeat was eaten. The weekly allowance of bread was two large loaves for each adult and one for each child. The bread itself was grey, tasted of chalk and increasingly unpalatable. Such was the poverty of the allowances, a League of Housewives was formed – led by Mrs Iris Lovelock, a vicar's wife from south London – and staged demonstrations and protests to improve the housewife's lot. Christine Fagg from Hertfordshire remembers how careful mothers had to be with food. 'I always cut an egg in half when I was frying it, so the children would have half an egg each. And I used to do the same with bananas. To this day, I will only eat half a banana and expect to give the other half away.'

Rural families were more likely to be self-sufficient and managed to avoid the worst of rationing by growing their own food, bartering and making the most of those things that were free in the countryside. John Harris was living near Newquay in Cornwall. 'We were never short of food. I grew onions, potatoes, turnips and carrots and supplied mother from the garden. During the winter there were flat-pole cabbages which were hung up in the back

RATION BOOK

SERIAL NO.

R.B.1
15

MINISTRY OF FOOD

1952-1953

RATION BOOK
(GENERAL)

Surname MORRIS Initials C.

Address 10 RHOSMAEN St LLANDILO

IF FOUND RETURN TO ANY FOOD OFFICE

FOOD OFFICE CODE No. Wa-D

BG 239726

Ration books were in use until 1954.

shed and mother would cut a piece off when she wanted. All the winter root vegetables, most of them went into stews and soups and that was our staple diet. Then you had summer vegetables, beans, peas, and potatoes again, a few lettuce and tomatoes and lots of spinach and cabbage. We kept poultry for eggs and killed them at Christmas. And there was a man down the road who'd slaughter the odd pig and give us offal for sausages. I supplied him with potato pickings and veg pickings for swill. Mother was over the moon to get the meat, as fresh pork was a real luxury. We lived off Cornish pasties a lot, and if meat was short it was filled with chicken or rabbit. And of course there was all the other food you could get, catching rabbits and picking apples and blackberries.'

In the towns and cities there were also ways of getting meat which didn't involve a butcher. Irene Ranahan was living in Bristol. 'We had chickens in the yard and when we didn't have any money we'd swap them for something else. I plucked chickens with my sister at Christmas, hanging them up outside and people would come and choose one. And then there was pigeon pie. Dad would knock out a few pigeons in the square, wring their necks and bring them home.'

There was enormous relief when rationing finally came to an end. Bread and preserves were derationed by the beginning of the fifties and tea in 1952. In 1953 the nation's children rejoiced as sweet rationing ended. Sarah Burton from Wolverhampton recalls, 'We went wild. The sheer joy of being able to go into a newsagent's and have a bar of chocolate all to yourself. I treated myself to a Mars bar every Friday. I still savour the taste of that treat

Meals more or less followed a set pattern during the fifties.

TY·Phoo
TEA

*The
Family
Favourite!*

Tea was de-rationed in 1952, the year that tea bags were launched.

today.' That same year sugar and eggs were derationed and in 1954 fats, meat and cheese came off the ration. At long last rationing books could be discarded.

In spite of the return of choice, meals more or less followed a set pattern in the early fifties with little left to the imagination. The mainstay of family meals was the Sunday roast. 'We'd have the roast on Sunday, leftovers hashed on Monday, Tuesday would be bubble and squeak, Wednesday was market day so there'd be something like boiled ham, Thursday was sausages and Friday was fish and chips,' recalls Eileen Cook, a housewife living in the Lancashire town of Colne. 'In fact we had chips that often – lunch would be fish and chips twice, then there was pie and chips, chip butties – it's a wonder we didn't turn into a chip.' A similar set menu existed for Maggie Stiles growing up in Leicester. 'Monday was cold meats left over from Sunday's roast, Tuesdays were liver and bacon, Wednesday fish and chips. It never changed, it was like "Oh, it's Thursday today, must be faggots and peas". It was a bit like the household chores – Monday wash day, Tuesday ironing, everything went to the same pattern.'

The most popular drink was tea. By 1957 its consumption had risen to a staggering average of six cups per adult per day (today we drink an average of around three cups a day). The nation woke up to a cuppa, it drank tea with every meal and 'everything stopped for tea' during breaks from work at eleven in the morning and three in the afternoon. Attempts by employers to abandon tea breaks were met with a smattering of 'tea break strikes'. Our favourite drink was chosen to mark almost every social occasion from birth to death, and if there was a crisis the first instinct was to take comfort with a cuppa.

With rationing over, the British started to become a little more adventurous. As a full range of products began to arrive in the country again there was a steadily increasing demand for new foods from overseas, like aubergines, courgettes, peppers and avocados. All this in a nation that had previously regarded the mushroom as exotic. Many people, though, were suspicious at first and the cookery queen Marguerite Patten recalls the confusion that was caused by avocados. 'They were called avocado pears. People thought they must be dessert pears like conference or William, something to eat after the meal and were disappointed by their unusual taste. It took a while to learn how to serve them.'

Meat was considered a luxury until the end of rationing, but became more widely available with the intensive farming methods of the post-war years. Twenty million broiler chickens were produced in the fifties alone and chicken became a part of the staple diet. Elsie Murphy from Liverpool recalls the transition. 'Before, we had never had much meat except for the occasional rabbit stew whenever we could get hold of it. Chicken had been for special occasions, something we had at Christmas and Easter. Now we were having it every Sunday.'

In the fifties it was generally thought that a girl could only catch a husband if she could cook. The way to a man's heart was through his stomach. But fourteen years of rationing had left a generation of women without the skills that were traditionally passed from mother to daughter. There was a feeling of panic as new housewives struggled to produce basic meals and many women went to night school to improve their cooking. Pamela Woodland from Rotherham had married in 1953. 'As a trainee teacher, we had people to cook for us so when I got married, I was at a loss. I couldn't cook, I got my first boiled egg thrown back at me. So I thought I'm intelligent, I should be able to do this. My mother bought me a Good Housekeeping cookbook and then I went to night school but it took time and confidence to learn to cook.' Joan Scott in Yorkshire felt it was a matter of necessity to attend classes in order to keep up with her newly married friends. 'We were all trying to outdo each other. I wanted to be the best amongst my friends so I went to night school to learn cooking for four or five years. And with so many new products coming in, you really had to do it.'

> ## CORONATION CHICKEN
>
> Coronation chicken was created in 1953 for the Coronation of Elizabeth II and was intended to appeal to the tastes and religions of her subjects throughout the Commonwealth and Empire. A simple recipe, consisting of cooked, chilled chicken in a mild curry mayonnaise sauce with apricots, it could be eaten on a tray so there was no need to miss a minute of the action on the new television sets that were bought to view the Coronation. The recipe became a firm summer favourite, particularly for parties.

Being a good cook wasn't just desirable; it was an essential part of being a wife. A young housewife would be expected to make dishes for her husband the way his mother used to – and, for the new bride, the test of her ability as a cook came the first time she invited her husband's family to dinner in her new home. The pressure would be on to live up to the daunting standards set by her mother-in-law. Having mastered the basics, women graduated to 'hostess cookery', a higher level of culinary skill which involved better quality ingredients and more sophisticated methods of preparation. It was characterized by its scrupulous presentation and love of decoration. Garnishes came into their own: orange segments on salads, hard-boiled eggs sculpted with piped mayonnaise, maraschino cherries on desserts. A knowledge of more sophisticated cuisine was especially important for the middle-class woman. Entertaining guests to dinner was one of her chief duties as a wife, and her status in the world was in part determined by her culinary ability. Having the boss to dinner was a rite of passage for a young couple who hoped to smooth the path of the husband's career by proving that they were 'the right kind of people'. And though it was his career enhancement that was at stake, it was her skills that were up for scrutiny. It was cooking for compliments and the biggest compliment that could be paid to the hostess was a request for the recipe of whatever marvel she had served.

Entertaining guests was one of the key social skills of the middle-class housewife.

THE HOSTESS *with the* MOSTEST

The world of home entertaining was very important in the fifties. Dinner parties were a chance to show off the modern features of the post-war house and present a perfect vision of middle-class family life. They were also highly competitive, as Sandra Fraye from Bournemouth discovered. 'We practised for them, it took days to prepare for one. All the wives used to try and outdo each other. You always had to offer two puddings and everything had to be presented perfectly, from the food to the table to the way you looked. Once I had the horror of having to chop a turkey in half because it wouldn't fit in the oven.' Now that servants were a thing of the past, the 'hostess trolley' came to the aid of the lady of the house, enabling her to serve food piping hot. Some trolleys were heated electrically, others had several layers which were kept hot by night lights placed underneath the serving trays. After serving drinks, which might include the new ladies' favourite – Babycham – the wife would disappear into the kitchen and re-emerge wheeling the trolley, possibly wearing a frilly affair known as a 'hostess apron' to protect her dress. The ultra-high standards even extended to social events amongst the wives themselves, as Sandra discovered. 'I was always off to coffee mornings where you had to wear a hat and look smart. The competition was fierce, women would try and outdo each other even down to the sugar lumps. You'd get them in different shapes and colours. I just couldn't keep up with it all.'

The cocktail party, an idea originally borrowed from the United States in the 1920s, also became a firm favourite and the cocktail cabinet had pride of place in the fifties front room. 'It lit up when you opened it and had all these cocktail sticks and a lemon squeezer,' remembers Dave Palmer, who bought one on hire purchase in 1959. Canapés were the chief nibbles, with vol-au-vents, cocktail sausages and pineapple and cheese cubes. Cheese and wine evenings became popular, taking advantage of the increasing availability of foreign cheeses from France, Denmark and the Netherlands and the new taste for wine. Marguerite Patten welcomed their arrival. 'First of all we'd got more cheese, remember for all those long years we had what we rather rudely called mousetrap cheese. Now we could actually choose cheeses and with the continental cheeses coming in, it was a voyage of discovery for many of us. And we'd only just started to drink wine in this country, and so we had a lot to find out about what wines went with which cheeses, but it was exciting and it was the first stage to easy entertaining.'

Wine was part of the food and drink revolution of the late fifties and sixties. The British were not only drinking more alcohol, they were becoming more discerning in their tastes – something that was particularly true of the new breed of wine-drinkers who discovered the pleasures of the grape on holidays abroad. Consumption doubled during the sixties as a new continental trend swept Britain: sipping wine with the evening meal. In 1960 Britons were drinking on average 3.6 pints of wine a year; by 1969, it was up to nearly 7 pints a year. The world of wines was, however, surrounded by snobbery. Those in the know quickly rejected the sweet white ones like Liebfraumilch that were favoured by the novices, many of whom came from an aspiring working-class or lower middle-class background. To order a dry white wine became a sign of 'class'.

The popularity of foreign food went hand in hand with that of wine, and rose in the sixties when millions of people began taking package holidays to

---

FASHIONABLE FOODS OF THE 50s

Hamburgers • Scampi
Ravioli • Mixed grill
Steak Diane • Quiche Lorraine
Puff pastry • Calves' liver paté
Vol-au-vents • Fish and chips
Crêpes Suzette
Lemon meringue pie

the Mediterranean. Until then olive oil had been something you bought at the chemist's but now, under the influence of cookery writers like Elizabeth David, it made the transition from medical cabinet to kitchen cupboard. For Irene Ranahan, mastering 'continental cookery' at night school was another way of proving her culinary sophistication. 'I made things like lasagne, boeuf Bourguignon which felt ever so swanky. Cooking in red wine was virtually unheard of, it was all meat and two veg up until then. I tried making spag bol using spaghetti, which was something we'd never had before, we weren't even sure how to eat it, with a spoon or a fork? But I couldn't quite stomach that Parmesan cheese, it smelt of sweaty socks.' The increase in immigration from the Commonwealth countries during the sixties also broadened the British palate. Margaret Maudsley of Blackpool became more experimental in the kitchen. 'I started making curries in the sixties and impressing friends by putting mango or sultanas in them. The first time I made a curry, I put so much curry powder in, it turned everything yellow. Even my curtains went yellow!'

Celebrity chefs started to emerge on television to guide people towards more adventurous cooking. Philip Harben and Marguerite Patten had made their debut on the box in 1947 and had agreed that he would be known as the first TV chef and she as the first TV cook. Marguerite, already familiar from her wartime work at the Ministry of Food, had a weekly television show throughout the fifties. 'I had to cater for all sorts. Some viewers wanted to return to the pre-war era and serve traditional British food. Young people, who now had their own homes but who had never had a chance to cook extensively due to rationing, needed basic information. And some who had lived or served abroad were keen to make their favourite foreign dishes.' The enthusiasm was such that Marguerite toured the country giving demonstrations to coachloads of cookery fans in town halls and theatres. Yolanda Sylvester from

Television cooks Marguerite Patten and Philip Harben show off their culinary skills to S E Reynolds (right) in 1950.

Hampshire was one of those in the audience. 'She'd stand at a big long table with all the chopping boards on it and because the ladies at the back couldn't see what was going on, they had a huge mirror on an angle up above her so that you could see her hands and watch her do the preparation from the back.' The cookery demonstrations were so popular that they soon turned into variety shows with audiences running into the thousands. Marguerite even shared the bill at the London Palladium with top stars of the time like Arthur Askey. 'At the big shows there would be dancers doing the cancan and an orchestra. I'd do my first spot of cooking and then we'd have perhaps a comedian and I'd be on again for my next session.'

As well as bringing us the chefs of the era, there were other ways in which television was influential in shaping the way we ate. When ITV was launched in 1955 it marked the start of television commercials that tempted people to consume new products. 'I bought a crinkle-cut chip cutter,' recalls Margaret Maudsley. 'I'd never thought of cutting my chips that way, but once I saw it on the television I thought it was the most sophisticated thing I'd ever seen. I had to have it.' As the new form of evening entertainment, television threatened the supremacy of the family evening meal when mother, father and children would sit down together to eat and discuss

With a TV dinner on a tray it was possible to eat without missing any of the action on the small screen.

the day's events. Books and magazines abounded with recipes for TV dinners that could be eaten from a tray across the lap so as not to miss the show. Some of these buffet-style eats were quite ambitious. Consider Fanny Cradock's suggestions for a TV-meal menu: dip 'n' dunk platter, baked mushroom cups, stuffed baked snails, chicken liver sauté, raspberry tartlets with orange cream sauce, iced tomato juice and a Chablis cup. In fact, a Mass Observation survey in 1957 showed that on average housewives with television sets spent half a day more a week preparing meals than those without.

SELF-SERVICE *and* SUPERMARKETS

The fifties and sixties saw a revolution in shopping for food, driven by the introduction of self-service. Shoppers were used to being served by shopkeepers in small stores on the high street and the neighbourhood corner shop. In the forties the Co-op tried 'pay as you go out' sections in its shops, and then in 1953 the Royal Arsenal Co-operative in London converted three shops into one in which customers helped themselves rather than asking the shopkeeper for items. Sainsbury's, too, was pioneering the idea of self-service and promoting it as 'Q-less shopping'. They had converted a shop in Croydon in 1950 and cleverly used tough, unbreakable perspex left over from wartime bombers as a means of protecting fresh food displays. Refrigerated cabinets meant it was easy to store perishable foods. By 1956 there were 3000 self-service stores in Britain. Six years later the number had risen to 12,000 and the new, bigger versions of these shops had been christened 'supermarkets'. By 1967 the figure was 24,000. Mary Greenhough recalls an early branch of the northern chain Morrison's in Bradford. 'It started as a corner shop and gradually expanded into a supermarket. I went in there with my son and he was amazed that you could just help yourself to anything from the shelves. "Yes, dear," I told him, "but you do have to pay for it afterwards."'

Self-service was a new idea that became the basis of the supermarket.

As shopping patterns started to change to self-service it became essential that products were attractively presented to catch the eye, and packaging became much brighter and colourful. Seductive wrappings launched new products like Ski yogurt and sugar-coated cereals such as Kellogg's frosted flakes in 1954. The fifties were also a time when products were presented in a variety of novel ways. Anchovy paste came from toothpaste-style tubes and dessert toppings were squeezed from the new aerosols.

The rise of the supermarket dealt a fatal blow to many corner shops, which for so long had been the linchpins of their communities. 'It was where you went to catch up with what was happening in the street,' remembers Eileen Cook. 'I was in there virtually every day, I'd always pick up something on the way home.' Although it only stocked a limited number of staples, the corner shop provided a personal service that the supermarkets couldn't match because of their sheer scale. Housewives were used to home deliveries from small shops like greengrocers. They would leave their order and it would be delivered by a boy on a bicycle within twenty-four hours, something that became a luxury in the last quarter of the twentieth century but was standard then. Shopping was more anonymous in supermarkets. No longer did shop assistants have time to chat with customers – they were too busy stacking shelves and working at the checkout.

The supermarket's main advantage over the corner shop was the range of food it offered. Irene Ranahan was bowled over by the one that opened near her home in Bristol. 'The Co-op was the crème de la crème. The vastness, the choice, you had everything there. There was all this fresh fish on display like Harrods, a counter with all the cheeses from around the world like you've never seen before in a corner shop, all this beautiful fruit from around the globe. Before I used to bring home melons from holiday, all there was back home was oranges, apples and pears. Now you could buy all these different varieties of fruit on your doorstep, and the amazing thing was that you could do all your shopping for the week.' Together with the refrigerator the supermarket reduced the regularity with which we shopped. It was possible to keep food fresh for much longer in a fridge than in a pantry. And in a supermarket you could do a big shop and take everything home in the car. From being a daily necessity, shopping for food became more of a weekly event.

Trex was one of the products housewives cooked with during the fifties and sixties.

IT'S OH SO CONVENIENT

In the sixties eating and shopping habits were significantly altered by the rise of convenience foods. This was linked to the sexual revolution, which saw women returning to the work place and wanting more in their lives than being stuck in a kitchen preparing meals. By the end of the decade convenience foods accounted for a quarter of the weekly shopping bill – women were too busy to cook everything themselves and buying pre-prepared food was a great way to cut corners. There had been a steady increase in the consumption of tinned foods during the interwar years but during the fifties advances in food technology and preservation methods had brought frozen foods into the shops in greater profusion. 'We had the first Bird's Eye frozen food cabinet in town,' says Margaret Maudsley, who was running a grocery in Kendal. 'All we sold were frozen peas and damaged chickens that the farmers would bring in. The peas were really popular, there'd be queues in the street for them.' Frozen peas were an instant hit, boosted by the string of shops that Bird's Eye opened. But they were soon eclipsed by fish fingers, which went on sale in 1955. Legend has it that they were originally going to be called 'frozen cod pieces' until someone pointed out the potential confusion. Sales of frozen foods doubled between 1955 and 1957 and by the early sixties a whole range of cheap ones, from vegetables to beefburgers, was readily available. And with fridge-freezers infiltrating the home, it was now possible to eat fruit and vegetables out of season.

FASHIONABLE FOODS OF THE 60s

Cheese straws • Prawn cocktail
Potted shrimps • Roast joints
Sole Veronique • Fondue
Coq au vin
Spaghetti Bolognese
Chicken Maryland • Paella
Pavlova • Black Forest gateau
Lemon cheesecake

'*The* BEST THING *Since* SLICED BREAD'

Sliced white bread was the ultimate symbol of convenience, produced and packaged on production lines that were the very opposite of the traditional bakery. The new bread was soft, slow to go stale and each slice was a perfect square. It was a boost for a nation used to the coarse grey national loaf of the wartime years. Pat Mancini in Manchester was sent down to the shops to queue up for one of the new sliced loaves ahead of the neighbours. 'The bread came all wrapped in paper, we showed it off in the street. No one could believe how many slices you got with it, people were looking at it like it was something from space.' For Christine Fagg in Hertfordshire, it was a

107

Instant mashed potato was one of a range of new convenience foods that saved time for the busy housewife.

godsend. 'It came as a bolt out of the blue, the greatest invention since the wheel. Nothing could solve the problems of having four young children like sliced bread. Before, you were forever hacking at a loaf with a half-blunt knife and now you could make sandwiches for the children with real ease, there were no more crumbs all over the kitchen floor, the children could help themselves, there was everything to commend it.' By 1969 Britons were eating forty-two million sliced white loaves a week.

Manufacturers originally targeted convenience foods not at working women but at the housewife-cum-hostess, suggesting that by using them she would have more time to beautify herself before her husband returned from work, or be ready for the worst eventuality – that he might unexpectedly bring the boss home with him. Although many women concealed the fact that they used labour-saving foods for fear of appearing to be less than perfect wives, Christine Fagg was a fan of them. 'Products like Campbell's condensed soup were great because you could put a mushroom or tomato soup over some cooked meat and get an instant sauce. It was marvellous to be able to open a tin and just dish it up – no washing up to do either. Rice pudding in tins was fantastic. Prior to that you would have to spend the whole morning in the kitchen making it, well can you believe the saving in time just opening a can and tipping the rice pudding out. The kids were just as happy with that as they would have been with an elaborate rice pudding that took all morning.' In 1954 Bird's Eye ran an advertisement for frozen vegetables stressing the economy of their produce: 'Not a ha'porth of waste with Bird's Eye. No stalks, leaves or pods to throw away.' Such an appeal to the housewife's sense of economy helped to assuage any lingering sense of guilt at using convenience foods rather than home-made ones.

With the rise of the working mother, people started to eat more informally in their kitchens. The next logical step for the family in a hurry was the ready-made meal, which made its debut in the sixties and hinted at a future of fast foods. Some of the bold, new dried and 'boil in the bag' foods ended up with cult status, like the Batchelor's Vesta curries which were launched in 1961. Aspiring housewives like Helen Hackney from Chester tried to pass them off as their own. 'I thought I'd try one of these new ready-made meals. "Just add water" to some meat. Well, it didn't look very nice, all dried up and there wasn't much of it either. I dressed it up with onions and a tin of pineapples hoping to make it look more appetizing. I hid away the packaging so that my husband would think I'd made it myself.'

Innovation also hit the drinks market. The desire for convenience extended to the country's top drink: tea. The tea bag was launched in 1952 and was vigorously promoted by Tetley's. 'When tea bags first came in everybody moaned and said, "Oh that's not proper tea it's just the sweepings",' remembers Bridget Redfield. 'Most people wouldn't use them but they soon became second nature to me. It meant I could make a cup of tea in a flash whenever I wanted one without having to empty the teapot, which would always be full of filthy old tea leaves which of course would go all over the sink and stain the sink.' The tea bag soon aquired three-quarters of the market for tea in the sixties. A similar development was happening in the world of tea's big rival, coffee. Nestlé first marketed its instant version, Nescafé, in 1960 and the brand quickly captured people's imagination. It was a convenience drink that fitted in nicely with the new hectic lifestyle, unlike the stronger European filtered coffee.

While tea and coffee were essentially adult drinks, children were indulged with more and more sweet, fizzy lemonade ones, often delivered door to door by 'the pop man'. John Gardner from south Gloucestershire remembers his weekly treat. 'The pop van used to come around on Wednesday afternoons. I would stand in the garden and wait for it to come around the corner. There was lemonade, dandelion and burdock, orangeade, but my favourite was cherryade. My older brother and I had to share the bottle. We'd pour out two glasses and make sure it was exactly the same amount in each glass. Then he'd encourage me to guzzle it down and taunt me with how much he had left, saying "Hmmm, this is really lovely".' The most popular brands originated as health drinks. Tizer, with its appetizer and cherryade brands, began production in Bristol in 1948, and Irn-Bru produced in Falkirk and Vimtonic from Manchester made similar claims to promote health and energy. With all things American being cool in the fifties, Coca-Cola and Pepsi Cola became synonymous with the new generation of teenagers.

R. White's was one of the brands of fizzy drinks loved by children.

109

Eating OUT

Eating out after the war was a real luxury, but the food was pretty grim even if you could afford it. For special occasions diners headed for a hotel restaurant, where they ate an expensive meal in snooty surroundings. It was in the 1960s that eating out became a popular and affordable pleasure, with the rise of international cuisine – the combined result of the advent of package holidays and immigration to Britain.

In the fifties the options were limited. Besides the posh hotel dining room, there were the department-store restaurants where you could have a light meal in between shopping, Lyons Corner Houses for a snack, and the greasy spoon, the caff where egg and chips was the most popular item on the menu. It was the teenagers who took to the idea of eating out on a regular basis. The cult status of all things American after the war – rock 'n' roll, Hollywood, heroes like James Dean and Elvis Presley – also applied to food. The ultimate food from the USA was the hamburger, and Britain's youngsters, who had seen teenagers in Hollywood films tuck into burgers, milkshakes and sodas, were ready to embrace it. Wimpy Bars provided the British version. The first one opened in 1954, serving hamburgers, cheeseburgers, grills and the Knickerbocker Glory. Every table came with a wipe-clean menu and the Wimpy icon: the ketchup bottle in the form of a plastic, squeezy tomato. It didn't take long for the bars to become a hit according to former managing director David Acheson. 'We realized that we were attracting an entirely new clientele – young people. The visual act of the chefs cooking your own personal order was very attractive. Soon there were permanent queues outside.' By 1969 there were 460 Wimpy Bars in Britain, with eight or nine alone in London's Oxford Street. 'They attracted a whole new tranche of customer – people who weren't used to eating out. They liked seeing the food being cooked, and knowing what they were in for. And having the menu in the window made it clear what it was going to cost.'

Meat was still a treat, even a status symbol, for many people in the fifties and sixties. The steakhouse was one option for a special meal to enjoy the culinary heights of steak served with chips, peas and mushrooms, and washed down with a nice bottle of wine. The Berni brothers went to the United States in the fifties to look into American steak restaurants and opened a chain of their own in Britain. The first Berni Inn opened in Bristol in 1953 and there were soon 150 nationwide, many of which breathed new life into historic pubs.

The lure of the Mediterranean cast its spell on package holidaymakers who returned home with an appetite for Continental food and a desire to eat out on a regular basis and not just for special occasions – the norm on the continent but out of the ordinary in Britain. Italian restaurants in the guise of spaghetti houses, pizzerias and trattorias were arguably the first wave of affordable foreign cuisine. The Latin spirit infused their atmosphere with candles in Chianti bottles and slushy music making them ideal for a romantic date.

The post-war immigration to Britain from Commonwealth and other countries brought with it a quiet food revolution that offered an experience of eating out that was light years away from the blandness of British cooking. Wherever there was an immigrant community, foreign restaurants and takeaways sprang up. Setting up a restaurant was initially a way of providing reassuringly familiar food and some comfort for immigrants, as well as a business opportunity for many new settlers who had to run the gauntlet of xenophobic attitudes in their search for employment. The Asian community, in particular, had a profound influence on the culture of eating out. Many of the Chinese immigrants ran laundries in Britain, but when they lost their trade to electric washing machines and coin-op launderettes, a large number turned to cooking and opened Chinese takeaways.

Indian restaurants were run mainly by Bangladeshis and started their passage into mainstream British life in the sixties. In 1960 there were only six in Britain. Ten years later this had risen to over 1200.

They were especially popular with cosmopolitan students who had been introduced to spicy foods on backpacking trips and were looking for cheap eats back home. The fact that the restaurants stayed open after pub hours made them popular for late-night meals. The macho challenge amongst drunken diners was to see who could eat the notorious 'vindaloo' – the hottest dish on the menu, it was far hotter than anything ever eaten by an Indian family. The rise of the Indian restaurant is one of Britain's most surprising success stories. The British embraced a cuisine that was far removed from suet pudding and roly-poly and once-conservative taste buds were won over. The curry house was a triumph, playing a significant and positive role in helping Indian immigrants towards integration. By the end of the twentieth century chicken tikka masala had become the most ordered dish in Britain.

Bathroom Additions and Modifications

JANUARY
1957

The PRACTICAL HOUSEHOLDER

Editor: F.J. CAMM

1'3

Home *Improvements*

THE FIFTIES AND SIXTIES, MORE THAN ANY PREVIOUS period, was the age when the design and furnishing of the home became an almost universal preoccupation. Houses and flats were more comfortable and convenient. They had mod cons and some even had central heating to provide constant warmth. New and fashionable leisure pursuits like hosting dinner parties and watching television meant that more time was being spent there. Now it wasn't enough just to have a home, it had to look good and boast the modern utilities. So attention turned to interior improvements and transforming bricks and mortar into the perfect modern home that reflected the style and standing of its occupants. DIY and decorating were the tools and they soon became a national pastime. The weekend wasn't for relaxing any more, it was a time for home improvements. And gardening also enjoyed a boom as gardeners turned their trowels from growing food to growing plants for pleasure, colour and fragrance.

The fifties brought a revolutionary new look into the home as vivid colours and new shapes arrived to brighten up a nation that was hungry for light and space after the drabness of war. It was called the 'contemporary look'. Rooms opened up, walls came down and light flooded in. Colours were primary, unnecessary decoration was taboo and shapes more angular. It was a world away from the dark and cluttered style of the previous generation. 'Everyone else was painting their kitchens cream and green but I wanted bright red and white in my kitchen,' says Rona Pettitt, who moved into a new home in Selly Oak, Birmingham, in the mid-fifties. 'It was the end of rationing and we really wanted brightness in our lives. We were finally able to buy things in different colours. During the war you could only buy brown teapots, now you could get them in any colour you liked.' The public first caught contemporary fever at the 1951 Festival of Britain, a showcase for the best in British art, science and design. The self-designated 'tonic for the nation' aimed to kick-start the post-war economy and inspired eight million visitors with its sample room settings in the Homes and Gardens pavilion. In a bid to encourage spending on home improvements, the government announced a tax-cutting budget in 1953 to kick-start a consumer boom.

By far the most significant home improvement for people in the fifties was the addition of a bathroom and indoor toilet. A survey in 1950 showed that nearly half of all British homes had no bathroom. That was the case for Eileen Cook from Lancashire when she married in 1950. 'We had to go down to my mother's for a proper wash and other than that you just got washed in the sink downstairs, which is where my husband had to shave. We had a toilet at the bottom of the yard. We were lucky enough to have a private one, some of our neighbours were sharing six families to a toilet. You really dreaded it when it was cold outside, sometimes it would freeze

SOUTH BANK EXHIBITION

LONDON

19 51

FESTIVAL OF BRITAIN
GUIDE PRICE 2/6

over. It was a bit creepy, you used to wait until the last minute before going and if it were dark you'd run down the yard with a candle which often as not went out.' Mary Greenhough from Bradford recalls some niceties that she observed. 'We used to cut up newspaper into squares and put a string through them to use as toilet paper. But when we had guests, we gave them tissue paper from the shoeboxes I got from work.' Many families, especially in the countryside, would dig holes in the garden in which to bury the waste. Gerry Burr from Somerset remembers, 'We had an outside loo which I'd empty in the front garden every night, it always seemed to happen around the time that one of the neighbours was passing by and would call out "Good evening".' Many people who went through this routine later discovered that they had mysteriously good crops of rhubarb.

For most working-class people cleanliness and a daily wash were important in the battle against grime and disease. Having a bath was usually a weekly event which involved bringing a tin bath in from the yard. 'We kept the bath on the roof of my sister's coal house and shared it with all the neighbours,' remembers Dave Palmer from Lancashire. 'Once a week I'd go around for it and I'd be walking along the street with a bath on my head and somebody would shout, "All right, Dave, must be bath night tonight". Every night the bath would be walking around the back streets on somebody's head or other. We called it the walking bath.' The bath was generally placed in front of the fire and each family member hopped in one after the other. 'Friday night was bath night,' recalls Ed Mitchell of Norfolk. 'We had a bungalow bath which was a long tin bath, I could just about sit in it with my knees out straight but before that we had an ordinary bath which Peg, my wife, used to do the washing in. To heat up the water we used to put the bath on the gas fire and light two burners underneath it and then Shirley used to be bathed first, who was then a little baby, then Graham was bathed in the same water, then we put in a couple of saucepans full of boiling water and it was getting a bit of scum on top by then and Peg would wipe the children down and get them into bed. Then Peg would get in the bath herself, put another couple of saucepans of water in and by the time I got into the bath, of course there was about an inch of scum in there and the water was

115

lukewarm.' The alternative to the tin bath was to go to the public baths for a scrub down, which is what Jim Finn did in Liverpool. 'I'd go with my mates to a wash-house on the corner of the street for a bath once a week. You'd wait until someone had finished and then go in there and wash it out with pink stuff before your turn. We'd be singing all the latest hits until someone would come along and threaten to throw us out if we didn't pipe down.'

To DIY *for*

The post-war generation were DIY pioneers. Before the war 70 per cent of families had lived in council or privately rented accommodation and had little incentive to improve their homes. Labour was cheap, so repairs were carried out by specialist tradesmen. The middle classes frowned on the idea of doing their own – it was something that only went on behind closed doors. But the war destroyed the stigma surrounding DIY as shortages and rationing forced the nation to forget social etiquette and make do and mend. Britons even tackled their first flat-pack challenge, in the form of the air-raid shelter, during the Blitz. After the war, home-ownership rose as the government embarked on a building programme to replace bomb-damaged houses and clear slums; and during the fifties and sixties some 2.3 million homes that had formerly been rented were sold for owner-occupation. However, in the early 1950s over a decade of neglect had left the nation's homes in urgent need of renovation and most professional builders were fully engaged reconstructing war-damaged Britain. As labour costs soared, few new home-owners could afford to get a man in, and there was no option but to do-it-yourself. An epidemic of home improvement swept the nation.

Ed Mitchell in Norwich was typical of those who took the plunge and, in 1955, put a deposit down on a family house. In order to save money he decided to tackle the installation of an indoor bathroom himself. 'To have my own property meant everything to me, but of course there wasn't a landlord to see to the jobs like painting and papering and, well, we didn't have a bathroom or an inside toilet. But through from the kitchen at the side was a kind of an archway and a fireplace beside it, so I knocked through from the kitchen into this room behind it which had been a wash house. I took the copper out and made that room into a bathroom, so now we had an indoor bathroom. But we still had an outdoor loo so I busted through from the bathroom into the loo and put a doorway in there. So now we had an indoor loo, indoor bathroom and I got a gas man to come up and put the

DIY became part of the modern marriage. Men did the heavier tasks while women chose patterns and colours.

The PRACTICAL HOUSEHOLDER

FEBRUARY 1961

1'3

Laying Decorative Flooring

Install a Picture Window
Easy to Build Fireplace

Teenager's Study Desk

gas geyser in over the bath, and I panelled it with hardboard and smartened it up and that was very good. It was going really upmarket to have an indoor bathroom. Just the thought of it was wonderful. To be able to walk in, open a tap and have hot running water and a nice warm bath. It was such a luxury after all that manhandling of a tin bath, filling it up and then toppling it over in the yard to let the water drain away.' During the sixties alone, the number of homes without a bathroom halved from 3.2 million to 1.5 million.

The hunger for DIY instruction led to a rash of new magazines in the fifties and sixties with names like *Man About the House*, *Practical Householder*, *Homemaker* and *Handyman* which encouraged couples to turn their home improvements into a labour of love. DIY was part of the modern marriage, a shared project to add value to a suburban castle and demonstrate a sense of style to friends and relations. Young couples spent their weekends making foldaway breakfast bars, fitting wood panelling and erecting porches. Husbands tended to do the heavier work with a drill or saw while women chose patterns and did tasks like wallpapering that demanded a finer touch.

After long years of austerity, fifties homemakers were at last given an opportunity to indulge their taste for colour and pattern. Margaret Maudsley in Blackpool went colour mad. 'When we moved into the flat above my hairdressing salon, we painted every cabinet door a different colour and every tile on the floor was a different colour too. We even covered the walls in heavy Anaglypta wallpaper and painted that.' By the mid-fifties manufacturers had begun to respond to demands from amateur decorators and produced a variety of bright paints with evocative names like avocado, vermilion, Aegean blue and jasmine yellow.

Wallpapers began to appear in vibrant, even clashing, colours and in distinctive lively designs. There was a fashion for using contrasting ones in the same room and manufacturers helped this along by producing matching sets. Pamela Woodland papered her house using the latest designs. 'One wall was dark green with red poppies on, another had an abstract fire design with yellow and tan flames crawling up the wall, I thought it would make the place feel warmer. I saw the poppy design in a hotel in Southsea and said to my husband, "I want that for our dining room," but when we saw it every day we soon realized that living with it was a mistake, so we changed it after about six months and kept changing the wallpaper until we found one we liked.' Other popular devices to enliven interiors included using strongly patterned papers to highlight certain areas such as an alcove or the

Isn't life COLOURFUL...

with clean-at-a-wipe FORMICA!

the surface with a smile

wall behind shelves. Subtle it was not. Wallpapering was for many the ultimate decorating challenge. Paste was made from flour and water, took ages to dry and often turned out lumpy, while the paper came with an edge that had to be trimmed – all of which added to the potential for disaster.

Formica was the buzzword of the age. The 'wonder' laminated plastic hailed from the USA, where two entrepreneurs discovered how to make a tough, heat-resistant covering from thermal-set resin-impregnated paper. Furniture could be covered with Formica and other bright new plastic laminates, injecting bold colours into even the dullest of rooms. 'We had Formica on the draining board, on the bath top, we had it on the coffee table,' remembers Jim Shaw from Derbyshire. 'It came in a wide variety of colours so you could match everything into your colour scheme. It was easy to cut, easy to apply, you could stick it down with contact adhesives. It was great. It opened up a world of possibilities for the home decorator.' The wipe-down working surfaces caught on and magazines praised them for not burning, scratching or staining. Irene Ranahan in Bristol was another convert. 'We covered everything we could with Formica, it was very, very fashionable and you didn't have to do anything with it. All you did was cut out the size that you wanted for your cabinets and stuck it on the top. You could do all sorts of things on it, you could slice your bread, cut your vegetables, it was virtually indestructible and you could just wipe it clean and it was beautiful. Your kitchen always looked so clean because of this Formica.'

The layout of the post-war home was a departure from what had gone before. New construction methods meant it was no longer necessary for modern houses to have internal load-bearing walls and so it was possible to make larger spaces. The parlour, a separate room once reserved for special occasions like Sundays, Christmas and displaying coffins, was a thing of the past. Living areas became more informal. Open-plan was the theme and rooms were increasingly dual-purpose – the kitchen/diner, for

Formica was the wonder substance of the era injecting bright colours into the home.

Opposite Wallpaper came in bold patterns with strong colours.

Kitchens became more comfortable places and were increasingly used as a place to dine as well as cook.

example. Built-in furniture helped to make the most of the space and multi-purpose shelving units acted as room dividers, often separating living and dining areas. The kitchen was no longer hidden away but was now a focal family room with fitted units, where a housewife could spend most of her time without feeling shut away. Central heating became increasingly common in middle-class households during the course of the sixties. Heating in bedrooms meant they were used for leisure as well as for sleeping and dressing. Radiators started to replace open fires, allowing a flexible furniture arrangement rather than one dominated by the need to have seating as close as possible to the fire.

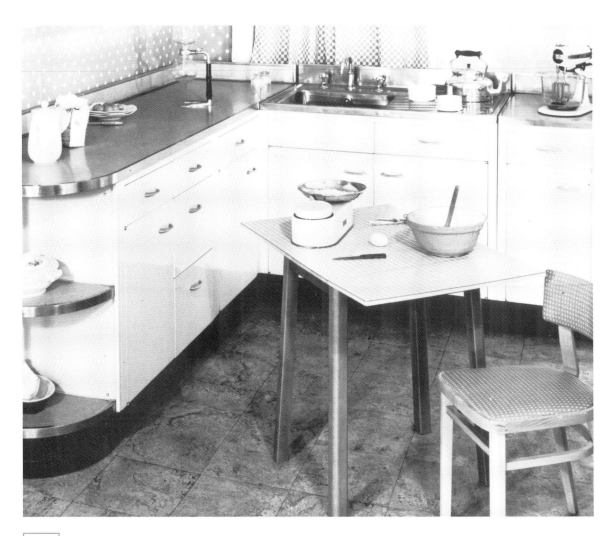

After the war, the scarcity of wood and other materials had meant that furniture was hard to come by. Availability was controlled by the government, who had launched the utility scheme during the war to provide basic standardized and price-controlled furniture for people who had been bombed out of their houses and for new homemakers. By necessity it was plain and functional, but it set a modern if conservative tone for furniture design once restrictions were lifted in 1952. G-Plan was one of the new ranges that brought the contemporary look into the ordinary home. Launched in 1953, this mass-produced furniture with its clean-lined Scandinavian style provided interchangeable units: 'to assemble, piece by piece, your own individual room arrangements.' Pamela Woodland had to have it for her home in Rotherham. 'G-Plan was all the rage then, to have it was a status symbol, everyone was buying it, a bit like Ikea now. I had a full suite of furniture in oak including a corner cupboard and a china cabinet. The chairs were quite functional and had these little legs on them but they weren't that comfortable, you couldn't sink into them and when a cold wind came under the door it shot up your legs!'

As the cult of DIY became ever more popular in the sixties, one man became its guru: Barry Bucknell, the first TV makeover star. Bucknell brought do-it-yourself to a mass audience through his television series in which he talked viewers through the basics of home improvements. In 1962 the BBC bought a derelict house in west London and Bucknell did it up in weekly episodes. The country watched and copied. Bucknell's fan mail started to outstrip even that of the *Coronation Street* stars, and when the BBC came to auction the house 2000 people a day turned up to view it. Barry Bucknell also played a part in shaping the nation's tastes. Modern was the keyword and hardboard was its tool. Out went the intricate period detail in Victorian and Edwardian houses and in came the hardboard to cover it up. Fireplaces were ripped out, picture rails and skirting boards disappeared and panelled doors were hidden behind the flat hardboard sheets. 'Doing a Bucknell' became a national catchphrase amongst DIYers.

By the mid-sixties it was clear that DIY wasn't just a passing fad; it was part of the fabric of life, stoked by glossy Sunday supplements. As one magazine put it: 'What was in the beginning an economic necessity, has now become a pleasurable pastime which brings profit to the pocket and self-satisfaction to many thousands.' The Ideal Home Exhibition was an annual pilgrimage for young homemakers looking for inspiration, and since 1957 a DIY exhibition had been held once a year at London's Olympia, bringing to the enthusiast wondrous new products like prepasted wallpaper, paint rollers and power tools.

Barry Bucknell was a DIY legend. His television appearances inspired millions of home-improvers and 'doing a Bucknell' became a national catchphrase.

The outside ROOM

The most influential, if unwitting, garden designer of the twentieth century was Adolf Hitler. Because of him British gardens were filled with Anderson shelters and rows of vegetables. Backyards were conscripted into the 'Dig for Victory' campaign. Lawns were ploughed up to grow food and city dwellers became amateur farmers, looking after chickens and pigs in their back gardens. Gardens were functional, not decorative, and flowers were regarded as an idle luxury. Everyone was expected to do their duty and the authorities employed officials to make sure it was vegetables, not flowers, that were being grown. Food went before beauty.

When the war ended the nation's gardeners were liberated from the monotony of growing nothing but vegetables, and Britons clamoured to fill their gardens with a riot of colour. 'We had very little choice then for the interior of the house, but I could get a lot of colour very cheaply from packets of seeds to produce this marvellous release from six years of drab living,' recalls Ivy Slade from Dorset. The flower that symbolized this new-found freedom was the rose, emblem of England and long-time favourite of gardeners. Peace, a golden-yellow rose with pink edges, had an almost mythical status and was said to be the last flower to be flown out of France before the Occupation. After the war it became the biggest selling rose ever, with nurseries working overtime to meet demand. It even had the royal seal of approval, with the Queen ordering six bushes.

The media face of the rose world was Harry Wheatcroft, a bewhiskered character who introduced a range of vibrantly coloured roses with exotic names like Pharaoh, Majorette, Safari, Maria Callas and Golden Shower. He was behind a Day-Glo hybrid called SuperStar that caused a sensation when it was launched in 1960. It was a vivid vermilion rose that brought glamour and fashion to the flower bed and the demand for it was so great that eager gardeners had to wait for up to two years to get it. In the new world of fancy gardening, creating the perfect bloom became an obsession. Advances in the science of genetics led

Roses were the most desired flowers of the fifties.

The alfresco lifestyle was inspired by the new fashion for foreign holidays.

to plant breeders offering a constant stream of new models and varieties.

The thirst for gardening information was satisfied by new programmes, magazines and books. *Gardeners' Question Time* was first broadcast on radio in 1947 and quickly became an essential for enthusiasts. On television it was Percy Thrower who was the face of gardening from 1956 with *Gardening Club*. His easy manner and homespun wisdom encouraged a new generation of gardeners. When he opened his own gardens to the public for the first time, over 9000 visitors turned up for a glimpse and the police had to reroute traffic.

In the sixties gardens opened up to continental influences. New affordable package holidays gave millions of ordinary people the chance to sit in the sun in Mediterranean countries and they came back to Britain with new ideas about open-air living and the alfresco lifestyle. With the addition of a 'patio', a word that originated in sunny Spain, the garden became an extension of the home, an extra room outside for sunbathing on a lounger and entertaining friends at a barbecue.

With the dawn of the age of leisure, gardening entered a new phase with recreation taking precedence over propagation. New gadgets that took the elbow grease out of the garden came on the market. Labour-saving devices such as battery-operated lawnmowers, hover mowers like the Flymo and petrol clippers took the hard work out of maintaining the lawn. However, the biggest innovation of all was the garden centre, first introduced in the early sixties. Garden centres made it possible to buy everything under one roof and plants came established in pots so that customers could see what they were buying. As one advertisement put it: 'Small plants, big plants, no need to wait for them to grow up nowadays. Just pick them up the size you want, complete with a trolley to cart to your car.' The era of instant gardening had arrived.

The SIXTIES PAD

In the sixties the home got groovy as all the rules were broken by a new generation that was liberating itself from the formality of its parents' functional furniture. The peacetime baby boom endowed the sixties with a glut of well-off teenagers – young people's wages had increased by 50 per cent in the early years of the decade. With this new-found financial independence, there was no need for them to wait for marriage in order to escape their parents' homes and there was an exodus to bedsit land and flat-sharing.

In sixties pads plastic was young and chic. It was cheaper than ever before and swamped the market to become the furnishing material of the decade. The invention of rigid foam plastic led designers to revel in its possibilities, with the moulded chair a must-have for the fashionable pad. Fun was another theme, as was furniture that moved with the times, and there was a brief vogue for inflatable furniture like blow-up armchairs which came with a puncture-repair kit. Disposables, from paper cups to cardboard chairs, were also groovy.

The space age was another influence on design. Sputnik-shaped bubbles appeared on chair and table legs, lamps resembled flying saucers and food mixers seemed to be modelled on nuclear warheads. 'I even had a Sputnik butter dish,' remembers Irene Ranahan, 'with spikes sticking out of it.' The lava lamp was the icon of the age and atomic power was seen as the key to a science-fiction future. At exhibitions designers showed off fantasies of a

Inflatable furniture enjoyed a brief vogue in the sixties.

futuristic home with robots doing all the chores. The 1956 Ideal Home Exhibition had a 'house of the future' with a waste-disposal unit, dishwasher and gamma-ray machine for treating foods. Sadly, the fully automated home never became reality.

One of the most influential designers and entrepreneurs in Britain made his debut in the mid-sixties. Terence Conran opened the first Habitat shop in 1964, declaring, 'We are the Mary Quant of the furniture world,' and brought the concept of the total lifestyle to a mass market. Habitat sold the whole package from furniture to crockery, lighting and kitchen equipment and offered good basic design to the young affluent middle class.

The CRASH PAD

Towards the end of the sixties, there was a growing disillusionment with the crass commercialism of modern society. Some people dropped out and headed off on the hippy trail, looking to older cultures for inspiration and to drugs for a quick fix. On their return home they tried new ways of living, such as in communes. The look of their homes changed, too, towards a laid-back style with the emphasis on living low, which was more practical for crashing out and taking drugs. Beanbags were scattered on the floor and ethnic artefacts, brought back from the overland trip to the east, provided the decoration. Psychedelia, inspired by mind-altering drugs, found its way into wallpaper designs, with disorienting, swirling patterns in pink, orange and purple cladding the walls of the funky pad.

At the end of the decade people were less inclined to go for the latest designs. Freedom of expression was in, and homes became as individual as their occupants. There was, though, a return to nostalgia with people raiding tips for Victorian and Edwardian furniture and Art Nouveau knick-knacks. The Biba emporium gave Victoriana a new status when it opened in 1964 and displayed clothes on Victorian hatstands and pieces of junk furniture; and street markets became the hottest places to shop for antiques.

In twenty years fashions in furnishings and interiors meandered through traditional, modern, space age, ethnic and psychedelic to nostalgic. What was fashionable might have changed but the desire to DIY was here to stay, laying the foundation for the modern obsession with home makeovers. Hardboard may have given way to MDF and Barry Bucknell to Handy Andy, but the basic British desire to improve the home is still going strong.

Week ending August 4 1956
Every Wednesday Fourpence

JOHN BULL

Begins this week
OLD FOURLEGS
My fantastic search for
the creature that lived
before the dawn of history
by Dr. J. L. B. SMITH

Miracle at Lensham
A long complete
story by
RICHARD DIMBLEBY

The **Battle** *of the* **Box**

I N THE LATE SIXTIES WATCHING THE BOX WAS FAR AND away Britain's most popular pastime. Shows like *Coronation Street*, *Match of the Day* and *The Wednesday Play* had become firm favourites with over a third of the nation. There were three television channels, which at the time seemed like a staggering choice and diversity. Some people were so hooked they spent more than thirty hours a week watching whatever was on. Yet back in 1950 the supremacy of television viewing was unimaginable to most people. The wireless was the most popular source of entertainment in the home and audiences for radio hits of the day like *The Archers* and *Mrs Dale's Diary* ran into many millions. In the early fifties very few homes possessed a television set and there was only one station: the BBC. Most people went to the cinema if they wanted to see moving pictures, and a battle developed throughout the fifties and sixties between the Bakelite, the big screen and the box.

Previous page Britain became hooked on television.

A 'Bush' Bakelite radio. The wireless was part of the background to family life.

As the fifties dawned the wireless was the king of home entertainment. 'The radio was on all the time, it was part of the background of family life, something we all shared,' remembers Chris Williams. 'We'd sit down to Sunday lunch and end up eating in silence because we were all concentrating on what was happening on the radio. I remember tapping my toes to *Family Favourites* and chuckling along to *Take It From Here*.' The BBC was a national institution, as revered as the royal family, and was listened to by virtually the whole country. It had begun broadcasting in 1922 and in the early days, under Lord Reith, its founding father, had attempted to instil high culture and a pious Christian morality. But it had gradually become more popular in its output. It was the wireless that had played a vital role during the war, bringing news and maintaining the nation's spirits. It was the best means of keeping in touch with the war effort and also the easiest way of escaping the horror of the conflict. In the fifties the challenge was to maintain the position of radio at the centre of people's lives. The BBC had created three networks – the Home Service, the Light Programme and the Third Programme – all of which kept to Lord Reith's principles to educate, inform and entertain. Each service broadcast plays, talks and music but they catered for different tastes. The Third Programme was the highbrow network with classical music and intellectual discussion, the middlebrow station was the Home Service with more news and speech-based programmes, and the Light Programme was the lowbrow one which played popular music. The idea behind this division was that the Third Programme was at the pinnacle of a pyramid, and that listeners would be gently encouraged to aim for its lofty heights by tuning in to the other networks and slowly learning to discriminate in favour of something more 'worthwhile'. That was the theory of self-improvement but the listeners thought otherwise. The Third Programme was destined to remain the least popular network while the lowbrow one, the Light Programme, captured two-thirds of the audience.

Throughout the day shows were aimed at the broad range of listeners. *Housewives' Choice*, one of the most popular programmes for women, went out after breakfast just when seven million housewives were sitting down to a cup of tea before getting stuck into the chores. *Music While You Work*, a wartime favourite, coincided with the mid-morning break for workers; and after lunch toddlers settled down to *Listen with Mother*, which started with the line, 'Are you sitting comfortably? Then I'll begin.' Older children looked forward to *Children's Hour* at five o'clock which featured, amongst other attractions, Toytown with Larry the Lamb.

Saturday afternoon was governed by *Sports Report*, when dad checked the football pools, and in the evening the main event was *Saturday Night Theatre*. Millions gathered around the wireless to listen to the plays, many of which were adapted from West End productions. Drama serials like *Mrs Dale's Diary* had a large following as did *Dick Barton, Special Agent* which at its peak was reaching audiences of over 15 million. The series was a huge hit with boys, amongst them Dave Palmer in Lancashire. 'When we were lads playing on the street everybody used to leave their doors open and all at once there'd be this particular tune, the Devil's Gallop, and then the announcer saying "Dick Barton". The whole street would empty in seconds literally. It was so exciting, the commentator would be telling you "Dick, Jock and Snowey are …". It drew you in because they got themselves into situations that you wished you could be in yourself.' The long-running soap opera *The Archers*, an everyday story of country folk, was conceived in 1950 as a 'farming Dick Barton', and was a means of informing farmers about new methods in agriculture through the easy-to-swallow pill of a rural radio drama set in the fictional county of Borsetshire. By the mid-fifties it was reaching way beyond the farming community to a staggering audience of twenty million who tuned in for their daily soap fix. Radio was universal listening. Jo Jones from north Wales was one of those hooked on the dramas. 'We relied a lot on the radio, we'd always listen to *Mrs Dale's Diary* and then it went off until *The Archers*. My uncle fixed some speakers up in my bedroom so that I could lie in the dark and listen to the plays. You used your imagination and you could picture all the characters, the pictures you built in your mind were so real.'

POPULAR RADIO PROGRAMMES FROM THE 1950s AND 1960s

• Listen With Mother •
• Housewives' Choice •
• Children's Hour • The Archers •
• Mrs Dale's Diary •
• Educating Archie •
• The Clitheroe Kid •
• Hancock's Half Hour •
• Any Questions • Beyond Our Ken •
• Brain of Britain •
• Billy Cotton Band Show •
• A Life of Bliss • Dan Dare •
• Dick Barton – Special Agent •
• Desert Island Discs •
• Down Your Way •
• Family Favourites •
• From Our Own Correspondent •
• The Goon Show • Have a Go! •
• I'm Sorry I'll Read That Again •
• In Town Tonight • Just a Minute •
• Music While You Work •
• Top Twenty • Ray's a Laugh •
• Record Review •
• Round the Horne •
• Saturday Night Theatre •
Saturday Night on the Light •
• Showtime from the London Palladium • Take It from Here •
• Top of the Form •
• Twenty Questions •
• Woman's Hour •

Comedy produced some of radio's biggest stars. *The Goon Show* made its debut in 1951, featuring the surreal humour of Spike Milligan, Peter Sellers, Harry Secombe and Michael Bentine. It was so anarchic there were attempts to take it off air. Tony Hancock of 23, Railway Cuttings, East Cheam, starred in *Hancock's Half Hour* from 1954. *Take It From Here*, featuring the Glum family, developed into a saga of working-class life. The sweethearts Ron and Eth were played by Dick Bentley and June Whitfield, with Jimmy Edwards' Mr Glum forever walking in on the couple.

The most popular of all the record request shows was *Family Favourites*, later *Two-Way Family Favourites*, which enabled families to keep in touch with servicemen and women abroad. The original billing read: 'From London, the tunes you asked us to play. From Germany, the tunes that make them think of you. Records played alternately.' Music was an important part of the output from Broadcasting House. The BBC ran thirteen orchestras and was Britain's largest employer of musicians, but there was one important musical trend that it ignored: rock 'n' roll. It was a mistake it was to regret.

The Goons – (*left to right*) Harry Secombe, Michael Bentine, Peter Sellers and Spike Milligan celebrate their success. After its debut in 1951, *The Goon Show* quickly attracted a cult following.

The BIG SCREEN

While the radio dominated home entertainment, it was the cinema that was everyone's regular night out. The Odeon, the Regent, the Gaumont, the Rank, the Granada, the Roxy, the ABC, the Rex, the Astoria, the Regal, the Real – every town had its local picture house. The cinema was the cheapest, most easily available form of mass entertainment. The perfect choice for a first date, it was somewhere warm and dark to experience the first fumblings of romance in a double seat in the back row. It was a window on to the world through films such as *The African Queen* (1951), *An American in Paris* (1951) and *Roman Holiday* (1953) and the latest fashions, passions and music from America arrived via the big screen. 'I used to go up to four times a week,' recalls Pat Dallimore from Bristol. 'It was the big night out, it was cheap, you'd meet all your friends at the pictures and it wasn't just the film either. There'd be the Pathé news, coming attractions, then a documentary on something. Often it was about other countries but once I saw one about the tobacco factory where I was working. Then there was the B film until finally we got the big film. I was a huge Robert Mitchum fan, I'd go and see him in anything. The cinema was pure escapism, you could lose yourself in it. It was uplifting, it was a different lifestyle. And when you came out you treated yourself to a bag of chips on the way home.'

A cinema queue in 1953. Many film fans went to the flicks several times a week.

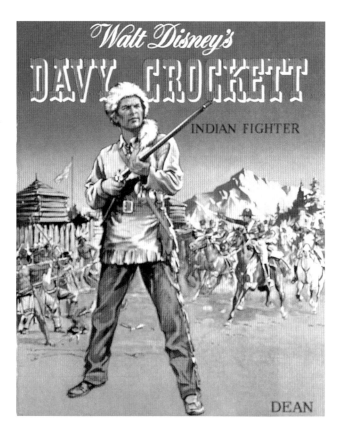

Walt Disney's DAVY CROCKETT INDIAN FIGHTER DEAN

Davy Crockett was a hero to millions of children. Young film fans would come to the cinema in buck-skin outfits and raccoon-skin caps.

Most cinema-goers started young with the Saturday morning trip to the matinee – the first half of the fifties was the golden age of Saturday cinema clubs. In 1950, 90 per cent of schoolchildren went regularly to the movies, more than half of them at least once a week. Youngsters queued around the block for Disney cartoons and live-action films like *Treasure Island* (1950) and *Davy Crockett, King of the Wild Frontier* (1956) – which captured the imaginations of millions of children. *Davy Crockett* turned into a phenomenon with boys and girls turning up to the main event in buckskin outfits and raccoon-skin caps. Mary Fitzsimmons got caught up in the craze in Sunderland. 'I made a hat out of my mother's real fur coat to go to see the film. My mother went spare but my father was over the moon with it and wore it down to the local pub.' The cinema club offered more than just the film and an opportunity to eat popcorn. Champions of the latest crazes like the Hula-Hoop and yo-yo gave demonstrations, and the atmosphere was boisterous with many children, especially older lads, running riot and shouting and chucking things at younger ones. In 1955 the weekly audience for the cinema clubs was over a million nationwide.

For adult cinema fans Hollywood reigned supreme. The hits of the fifties ranged from musicals like *High Society* (1956) to comedies such as *Some Like It Hot* (1959), westerns including *High Noon* (1952) and steamy dramas like *From Here to Eternity* (1953). Screen stars included blonde bombshell Marilyn Monroe, the cool hero James Dean, Elizabeth Taylor, Marlon Brando, Jayne Mansfield, Debbie Reynolds, Rock Hudson and girl-next-door Doris Day. 'My friend loved Doris Day so much she went to see *Tea for Two* twenty times all over town,' remembers Irene Ranahan. 'All the boys idolized John Wayne, but I really liked Debbie Reynolds, she had such a sparkle, I even named my daughter after her. When you went to the cinema you felt you were entering this world of beautiful people in marvellous clothes. You wanted to be like the stars.' Cinema-goers were able to keep up with the antics of their favourite stars through the abundance of film magazines like *Picturegoer* which gave a glimpse into their idols' glamorous lives.

Life CAN NEVER BE THE SAME

'If you let a TV set through your front door, life can never be the same' – *Daily Mirror* (1950). While the big screen dominated nights out, the small one was making inroads into people's lives and vying to take over from the cinema and radio as the number one form of family entertainment. It was Elizabeth II's coronation in 1953 that ushered in the era of the box. Although television came into existence in the 1930s, sets were prohibitively expensive – they cost the equivalent of several thousand pounds – and the number of viewers who could tune in were limited to people living in London, Birmingham, Cardiff, Glasgow and Manchester. After the war, manufacturers started to make cheaper sets, but even in 1950 only a mere 350,000 householders could watch television.

The Coronation made all the difference. It was the most spectacular state occasion for decades and the first mass televisual event. No one wanted to miss out on it and the days leading up to it saw sales of

---

1950s FAVOURITE FILMS

1950: Sunset Boulevard; All About Eve;
Annie Get Your Gun
1951: A Streetcar Named Desire;
The African Queen; An American in Paris;
Strangers on a Train; The Lavender Hill Mob;
The Man in the White Suit
1952: Singin' in the Rain; High Noon
1953: From Here to Eternity;
The Wild One; Gentlemen Prefer Blondes;
Genevieve ; Roman Holiday
1954: On the Waterfront; Rear Window;
Dial M for Murder; One Good Turn;
20,000 Leagues under the Sea
1955: Rebel Without a Cause; East of Eden; The
Seven Year Itch; The Ladykillers;

Blackboard Jungle; Oklahoma;
Guys and Dolls; The Dam Busters; Richard III
1956: Around the World in Eighty Days;
The King and I; High Society;
Forbidden Planet; Reach for the Sky;
The Ten Commandments; Giant;
Rock Around the Clock; Love Me Tender
1957: Bridge on the River Kwai;
Jailhouse Rock; Twelve Angry Men;
Lucky Jim; Pinky and Perky
1958: Vertigo; Carry On Sergeant
1959: Some Like It Hot; Ben Hur;
Look Back In Anger; North By Northwest;
I'm All Right, Jack; Room at the Top;
Our Man in Havana

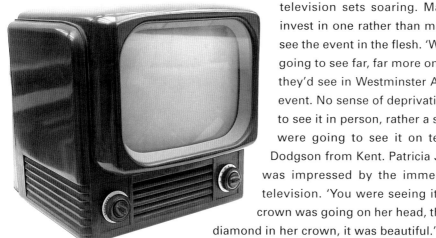

The days leading up to the Coronation in 1953 saw the sales of televisions soaring.

television sets soaring. Many people preferred to invest in one rather than make the trip to London to see the event in the flesh. 'We were told that we were going to see far, far more on television than anything they'd see in Westminster Abbey. We were in on the event. No sense of deprivation that we weren't going to see it in person, rather a sense of privilege that we were going to see it on television,' recalls Sylvia Dodgson from Kent. Patricia Johnstone in Lanarkshire was impressed by the immediacy of watching it on television. 'You were seeing it as it happened. As that crown was going on her head, the sun suddenly caught a diamond in her crown, it was beautiful.'

On 2 June 1953 over twenty million people in Britain saw the Coronation on television. The BBC estimated that around eight million watched it in their own homes, another ten million were in the homes of friends and neighbours and around two million saw it in pubs and cinemas. In that year alone, 100,000 television sets were sold and Britain's skyline underwent a transformation as thousands of H-shaped aerials went up on roof tops next to soon-to-be-redundant chimney pots. The atmosphere of the living room also changed. The fireplace was no longer the focal point of the room, it had been usurped by the television set. At first many people felt ashamed of owning one – they thought it was somehow common – and hid it in a cabinet or surrounded it with book shelves to disguise it.

Many amateurs applied their rudimentary knowledge of physics to making their own sets. Christine Fagg's husband rose to the challenge. 'He took a 6-inch tube and an old air-force radar to put it together. It was absolutely minute with all shades of green, you couldn't really see much, we used to crouch around to watch it, and your eyes ached like hell afterwards. But it had a magnetic power and all our friends would come around to stare at it!' The DIY spirit extended to Graham Bill's father, from Staffordshire who spent a lot of time perched precariously on the roof. 'We had a 12-inch screen, which was quite a status symbol, but there was no aerial. Why it was missing, I never knew, but Dad made an aerial out of copper tubing and climbed on to the roof to fix it to our chimney whilst we watched the picture and shouted to him when the reception was acceptable. This worked until high winds came and the whole process had to be repeated – regularly.'

Reception was a problem for most viewers and the BBC received numerous complaints about snowy-white pictures. Even television sets fresh off the factory line required hours of attention to get them working properly. A lot of interference was caused by cars driving past houses and motorists were advised to fit suppressors to the ignition in their vehicles to get around the problem. 'When a set went wrong, it was a tragedy, like a death in the family,' recalls Gerald Wells, a television repairman throughout the fifties and sixties. 'Sometimes when I arrived on a street with my box of tools, a cheer would go up that I'd come to fix the set. They'd willingly fork out whatever it cost to get it working again. It made me feel terribly important. Being a repairman then was a bit like being a doctor, you were treated with the same respect. You'd put right a friend of the family that was ill.'

The Coronation had been a communal experience and this became the pattern for television viewing, with friends and neighbours crowding into the nearest house that had a set. Jo Roffey was lucky enough to have one at home in Streatham. 'It was such a tiny screen, there was a magnifier in front of it so that you could see better. We would wheel it into the living room and then there'd be this "knock knock" on the door. The first programme was five o'clock – *Children's Hour* – so all the kids would knock at the door and they'd all be standing at the back because we never had enough seats for

---

1950s FAVOURITE TELEVISION PROGRAMMES

1950: Andy Pandy; Come Dancing
1951: What's My Line
1952: Bill and Ben the Flowerpot Men; Animal, Vegetable, Mineral?; Panorama
1953: The Coronation; Rag, Tag and Bobtail; The Quatermass Experiment
1954: Zoo Quest; Lassie
1955: Crackerjack; Dixon of Dock Green; Double Your Money; Benny Hill Show; The Grove Family; Sooty; This Is Your Life; The Brains Trust; The Woodentops

1956: Hancock's Half Hour; Whack-O!; What the Papers Say; Zoo Time; Eurovision Song Contest; Opportunity Knocks
1957: Tonight; Emergency Ward Ten; Captain Pugwash; Six-Five Special; The Sky At Night; The Phil Silvers Show
1958: Blue Peter; The Larkins; Beat the Clock; Oh Boy!; Educating Archie; Grandstand; Black and White Minstrel Show
1959: Juke Box Jury

everyone to sit down. But it even happened with the grown-ups. If our relations came round they used to sit in rows to watch the box.' Tony Holt from south London remembers being an uninvited guest when a television set arrived in his street. 'It belonged to the Hewitts, they were a better-off family who lived across the road. I used to sneak into their front garden with my mates, hide in the dahlias and watch the TV through the window. We were fascinated even though we couldn't hear anything. If they had looked round, they would have seen all these heads popping up with bulging eyes staring at this magic box.'

Hours of viewing were restricted – the BBC transmitters switched on at 3 o'clock on weekdays and 5 o'clock on Sundays, and closed down between 6 p.m. and 7 p.m. for the toddlers' truce, when children were led to believe that the entertainment was over so that mothers could put them to bed. This collusion between parents and the BBC continued until 1957. For adults, television was an evening activity to be enjoyed at the end of the day. The tone was sophisticated – announcers wore evening wear and the well-spoken female ones were models of deportment. There were frequent interludes between programmes when the screen would be filled with soothing images like a revolving potter's wheel, waves crashing on rocks, horses ploughing or a windmill turning.

The children of the fifties were the first television generation. 'It was very special,' remembers John Gardner from south Gloucestershire. 'I'd sit down with my mother for *Children's Hour* from five until six. We usually had a jam tart and a glass of milk. There were all these puppet programmes like *Muffin the Mule*. You could see the strings pulling the puppets but it didn't seem to make any difference, you still thought they were real. There was a different one every day. On Tuesdays there was *Andy Pandy*, Wednesday was *The Flowerpot Men*, Thursdays meant *Rag, Tag and Bobtail* and on Fridays there were the *Woodentops* who lived on a farm with Spotty the dog.' Other puppets to make it big were Sooty, who first went on the air in 1956 with his sidekicks Sweep and Soo, and, in the following year, Pinky and Perky. 'It's Friday, it's five to five' meant that it was time for *Crackerjack*, which started in 1955. There was a quiz called 'double or drop', and toys and games were given for correctly answered questions. The reward for a wrong answer was a cabbage. The BBC's flagship children's programme, *Blue Peter*, started in 1958 and the presenters Christopher Trace and Leila Williams encouraged young viewers to learn new skills and make useful things out of egg cartons, cardboard boxes and sticky-back plastic.

The children of the fifties were the first TV generation. *Children's Hour* began at 5 p.m.

In the early days the BBC really was Auntie and gave adult viewers programmes with a strong educational flavour. There was advice on gardening from Fred Streeter, cookery lessons from Marguerite Patten and Philip Harben and music appreciation presented by Eric Robinson in *Music For You. Dixon of Dock Green* introduced the first television copper in 1955. PC George Dixon was the old-fashioned bobby on the beat who greeted viewers to each episode with 'Evening all'. The first soap was *The Grove Family*, so named because it was transmitted live from the BBC's studios at Lime Grove. It documented the goings-on in the lives of builder Bob Grove and his suburban family. Fun came in the shape of panel games like the American import *What's My Line* which started in 1951. One of the panellists, Gilbert Harding, a former schoolteacher with a crotchety, gruff manner, bow tie and moustache, was destined to become Britain's first television-bred star. He was a British institution, in constant demand for his opinions, to write newspaper articles and make public appearances.

Marguerite Patten experienced the transformation from radio star to television celebrity whose face was recognized nationwide. 'There was something very intimate about those early days of television. People would stop me in the street. I'd be coming out of the grocers and it was, "Oh, you're Marguerite Patten". I was so staggered because that happened a lot in the fifties and they were very funny, our viewers, they'd make comments like, "Oh, Marguerite, I don't like the way you've done your hair this time, go back to the other way". Or "That's a very pretty dress Marguerite, can you tell me where you bought it?"'

Watching television was a special event, a bit like having a private cinema. One of the attractions of the picture palace had been that it took people out of their living rooms and into its splendours. The little black box reversed the process, bringing people back into their homes which, with central heating and other creature comforts, were by now a good deal more pleasant. 'There was an excitement in the stomach about what we were going to see, a sense of occasion,' remembers Maureen Gilbey from Southampton. 'We'd have our tea early and tidy everything away. All the furniture was rearranged to face the TV, the curtains drawn as we sat down to watch. There were so many good programmes on, it was much easier and cheaper to stay in with the television than pay out for a babysitter while we went to the pictures.' By the end of the decade television was available to more than 95 per cent of the UK population.

The BIG SCREEN *fights back*

In the mid-fifties Hollywood was starting to wise up to the competition it was facing from television. In order to fight off its black-and-white rival, it made more films in colour and experimented with new techniques like 3-D and panoramic screens like Cinemascope with stereophonic sound. Big screens meant big themes and Hollywood produced Biblical epics with chariots, casts of thousands and, it seems inevitably, Charlton Heston in films like *The Ten Commandments* (1956) and *Ben Hur* (1959). There was no way the small screen could produce anything to compare with the sheer size and spectacle of the blockbuster.

British cinema was keeping the competition at bay with home-grown comedies like *The Lavender Hill Mob* (1951) from Ealing Studios. The bawdy humour of the *Carry On* films had audiences rolling in the aisles from 1958 when the first one, *Carry On Sergeant*, was released. The slapstick comedy and smutty jokes tickled the nation's funny bone and made stars of the regular cast of Sid James, Kenneth Williams, Hattie Jacques, Joan Sims, Barbara Windsor and Charles Hawtrey. The laughs kept on coming with a total of eighteen *Carry On* films between their debut and *Carry On Again Doctor* at the end of the sixties. The other comedy

Ben Hur (1959) was a hugely popular Hollywood biblical epic that featured Charlton Heston, chariots and a cast of thousands.

series that was a box-office success was the *Doctor* films starring Dirk Bogarde as Simon Sparrow. It got off to a flying start with *Doctor in the House* in 1954, which was immediately followed by *Doctor at Sea* (1955) and *Doctor at Large* in 1957.

With television making an impact on cinema audiences, the film industry shifted its focus to the one group that was still keen to go out and have fun – teenagers – and reflected the strong youth culture of the time through films like *Rebel Without A Cause* in 1955 which had James Dean capturing the rebellious spirit of young people, as did Marlon Brando in *The Wild One* (1953). The first real teenpic was *Rock Around the Clock* (1956) with Bill Haley.

Elvis Presley, the pin-up of the day, starred in a series of teenpics beginning in 1956 with *Love Me Tender*. Jo Roffey was a love-struck teenager when she first saw her idol on film. 'I couldn't get over how handsome he was, there was no one to touch him. At first Elvis films were shown in the West End so we'd all go up there on the bus, but then they started showing them at the local cinemas so we used to go every night. Didn't just see the film once, we used to go every single night. I knew the films word for word from beginning to end. We'd all get up and dance in the aisles and of course down would come the old manager, hollering and shouting.

Rock 'n' roll was also having an impact on the wireless. Its rise coincided with the arrival on the high street of more compact transistor radios. They were light and convenient, and teenagers took to them immediately. It meant they could listen to their own shows and avoid their parents' choice. At the time, though, there weren't many programmes on BBC Radio that appealed to teenagers – rock 'n' roll was considered to be a passing fad. Anyone who wanted to catch the new music had to search it out on commercial stations like Radio Luxembourg whose Top Twenty on Sunday nights gave young people what the BBC wouldn't. 'It was always fading in and out but that didn't put me off listening,' remembers Adrian Flint in Warwickshire. 'My dad wouldn't let me listen to the radio in the evening, so I built a crystal set and listened to Radio Luxembourg under the sheets.' John Gardner also tuned in from under the bedclothes. 'I desperately wanted a transistor radio and got one for my birthday. I'd snuggle up in bed and listen to Luxembourg in the dark. If there was a song I really liked, I'd turn it up louder. Sooner or later mum would holler out "Turn that music down, you're supposed to be asleep". Of course my parents hated Luxembourg because it played nothing but pop music, but I thought it was great.'

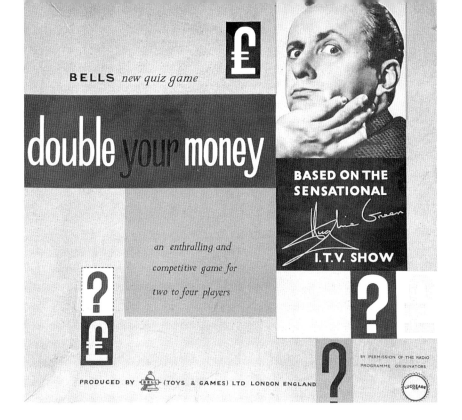

'THE *other* SIDE'

It wasn't only on the radio front that the BBC was facing competition. In 1955 its first-ever rival appeared when commercial television made its debut. The launch issue of *TV Times* declared that, 'Viewers will no longer have to accept what is deemed best for them. The new independent television planners aim at giving viewers what viewers want – at the time viewers want it.' Programmes were made to accommodate advertisement breaks and ITV brought more game shows and variety shows to the screen. BBC Radio managed to steal its thunder on its opening night, 22 September 1955, by broadcasting a momentous episode of *The Archers* in which one of the characters, Grace Archer, died in a fire. At first, only 190,000 homes could pick up the commercial transmissions and the rate at which people converted their sets was leisurely, but within a few years ITV was regularly gaining an audience share of up to 70 per cent, more than giving the BBC a run for its money.

The biggest ITV hits in the fifties were *Double Your Money*, *Take Your Pick* and *Sunday Night at the London Palladium*, an all-singing, all-dancing extravaganza featuring the variety stars of the day and hosted from 1958 by Bruce Forsyth. From the start ITV established itself as the channel for unashamedly populist fun and entertainment, whereas the BBC was seen as being much more elitist and prescriptive. The commercial channel brought ordinary people on to the screen, which had previously been the

Double Your Money, hosted by Hughie Green, had begun on Radio Luxembourg before transferring to ITV in 1955.

preserve of the great and the good. There was initially a lot of resistance to it, particularly from middle-class families. 'We weren't allowed to watch ITV,' recalls Susan Howe from Berkshire. 'My mother was a teacher and she thought it would somehow rot our brains.' *Opportunity Knocks*, which ran for two decades from 1956 and reached audiences of up to twenty-five million, embodied the appeal of ITV. It was television for the people by the people. Hughie Green hosted this amateur talent contest, adopting the guise of an American game-show host. The 'clapometer' in the studio gave an indication of the most popular act but the eventual winner was decided by the viewers at home who cast their votes by post.

A choice of channels was bound to lead to family conflict over who got to choose what to watch. In Jo Jones' home in north Wales it was her father who was in control of the switch. 'He was a sports addict and my mum wasn't interested, so we knew if there was sport on there was going to be a silence from Mum because Dad would switch on the football and she would sit there clacking her knitting needles so that he couldn't really enjoy it. She preferred the plays and documentaries. One thing we always had to watch was the church service on Sundays. I was supposed to sit still, but I didn't mind because it meant that I didn't have to go to church on Sunday evenings and it was a lot warmer to sit in front of the television. If ever Cliff Richard came on, I just had to watch him or any of the pop shows. Dad thought it was a noise and, at first when there was only one channel, it didn't really matter, but when we got two channels and there was sport on the other side I always lost out.'

AND NOW *for a* SHORT BREAK

The arrival of commercials on television was heralded as an evil invasion of British life that would somehow corrupt the viewers. The commercial channel, funded by advertisements, had only been allowed on the air after a long political battle. In the event the first advert, for Gibbs SR toothpaste – 'It's tingling fresh. It's fresh as ice' – didn't lead to brainwashed viewers stampeding towards the chemist, but there were still complaints about the intrusiveness of the commercial break. The protests eventually died down and some advertisements created characters with an enduring appeal such as the Oxo family, the Dulux dog and the PG Tips chimps. Slogans passed into the national consciousness: Beanz means Heinz; Murray Mints – too good to hurry mints; For hands that do dishes; All because the lady loves Milk Tray. Of course, what was a commercial break for some was a tea break for others and the national grid had to prepare for a power surge during advertisements.

By 1959, 60 per cent of British adults were tuning in every evening for up to five hours in winter and three and a half in summer, and concerns were voiced about children's viewing habits. It was estimated that the average child watched television for around two hours a day and this new habit ate into other activities like reading, homework, listening to the radio and playing with friends outdoors. The biggest casualty of television was the film industry. In 1950 cinema-goers had brought in 1400 million admissions. Commercial television began late in 1955 and from 1956 to 1960 attendances more than halved, dropping to only 500 million admissions in 1960.

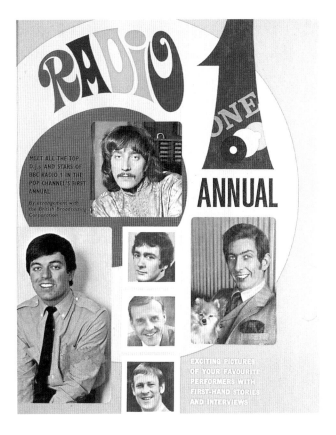

ALL *at* SEA

In 1957 television licences in Britain overtook radio ones for the first time and the downturn in radio audiences compared to television viewers accelerated in the sixties. However, there was one area in which listening to the wireless was booming, although illegally. Pirate radio stations took off and became a sixties phenomenon. They operated offshore, outside the law, with DJs playing the pop music that the BBC was largely ignoring. Veronica, anchored off the coast of the Netherlands, was one of the first in 1961, but the most well-known was Radio Caroline which broadcast from a ship in the North Sea from 1964. By the end of 1965 the pirate stations had around 15 million regular listeners and it was estimated that 45 per cent of the population listened to either an offshore station or Radio Luxembourg. The pirates posed a safety risk for shipping because they disrupted normal maritime communications, and were effectively shut down by the Marine Broadcasting Offences Act in 1967. This was seen as censorship by some listeners but the BBC was quick to step in and launch its own pop network on 30 September 1967. Radio 1. At the same time, all its radio networks had a makeover. The Home Service became Radio 4, the Third Programme changed to Radio 3 and the Light Programme became Radio 2.

Radio 1 was launched on September 30, 1967. Tony Blackburn was the first DJ to present a show on the station.

Coronation Street arrived in 1960 and went on to become ITV's top-rating show.

In the sixties the cinema again looked to the youth market to hold on to its audience in the face of the growing dominance of television. Hollywood brought out youth-oriented and counterculture films in the shape of *Easy Rider* (1969) and *Bonnie and Clyde* (1965) and they were big hits. There were also home-grown Swinging London films like *Georgy Girl* (1966), *Darling* (1965), *The Knack* (1965) and *Alfie* (1966). 007, James Bond, charmed cinema-goers with his devilishly chauvinistic ways and made a huge impact on cinema audiences of all ages worldwide, starting in 1962 with the box-office hit *Dr No*. This was quickly followed by *From Russia With Love* (1963), *Goldfinger* (1964) and *Thunderball* (1965). However, it couldn't reverse the trend towards television and people preferred to stay in the comfort of their own homes watching the box rather than venturing out to the cinema. In 1950 there were around 4500 cinemas in Britain; by 1967 this had dropped to 1800. In desperation, films were made of television shows like *Thunderbirds* (1966) and *Till Death Us Do Part* (1969), but it was too late to stop the rot.

Television built on its growing ascendancy in the sixties by increasing the range and quality of its programmes. There was a new sense of realism with the portrayal of more ordinary lives. A gritty view of life in Britain came through in BBC plays like *Up the Junction* (1965), *Cathy Come Home* (1966) and ITV's *Armchair Theatre* (1956–74). *Z Cars*, which started in 1962, was a more realistic cop show than the rose-tinted *Dixon of Dock Green* and the comedy *Till Death Us Do Part* introduced Warren Mitchell as an antisocial working-class bigot. Mary Whitehouse targeted the show as part of her 'Clean Up Britain' campaign, keeping a tally of its bad language. *Coronation Street*, on air from 1960, provided a fictional insight into life in the down-to-earth terraced streets of Salford. The characters were familiar to the viewers –

everyone knew an Ena Sharples, Elsie Tanner, Hilda Ogden or Len Fairclough. By 1965 it had become the nation's favourite show.

The sixties also saw the emergence of high-quality satirical television. The Establishment would never be seen in the same light again after the arrival in 1962 of David Frost and the *That Was the Week That Was* team which included Michael Crawford, Millicent Martin, Kenneth Cope, David Kernan, Bernard Levin, Lance Percival, Roy Kinnear and Willie Rushton. More anarchic stars were waiting in the wings – *Monty Python's Flying Circus* (1969) was equally ground-breaking in its pioneering of a new form of surreal comedy.

Youth TV was also expanding with *Juke Box Jury* (1959–67), *Six-five Special* (1957–58), *Ready Steady Go* and *Top of the Pops*. 'You could see the pop groups who played the music we were listening to,' remembers Annie Hughes from Chelmsford. 'It was tremendously exciting. Pop music came to us through the television, you saw what the fashions were too so that you could keep up with them.' Science fiction was cult viewing amongst the teens with *Doctor Who*, *The Twilight Zone* and *Star Trek* leading the way to the final

1960s FAVOURITE FILMS

1960: Saturday Night and Sunday Morning; Spartacus; The Apartment; Psycho; Sons and Lovers
1961: A Taste of Honey; Breakfast at Tiffany's; The Magnificent Seven; Swiss Family Robinson
1962: Lawrence of Arabia; Dr. No; The Loneliness of the Long Distance Runner; The Guns of Navarone; The Young Ones; A Kind of Loving
1963: This Sporting Life; Cleopatra; From Russia With Love; The Great Escape; The Birds; Tom Jones; Billy Liar
1964: Dr Strangelove; A Fistful of Dollars; Goldfinger; Mary Poppins; Zorba the Greek

1965: Darling; Dr Zhivago; Thunderball; The Sound of Music; Bonnie and Clyde
1966: Alfie; The Good, the Bad and the Ugly; A Man for all Seasons; Georgy Girl; Those Magnificent Men in their Flying Machines
1967: The Graduate; The Dirty Dozen; Jungle Book; In the Heat of the Night
1968: Chitty Chitty Bang Bang; Barbarella; 2001: A Space Odyssey; Carry On Camping; Oliver!; Rosemary's Baby
1969: Butch Cassidy and the Sundance Kid; Midnight Cowboy; Easy Rider; The Virgin Soldiers; Bob and Carol and Ted and Alice

frontier. Chris Williams was a fan of a sci-fi classic: 'I loved *Quatermass and the Pit*. It was a really gripping tale of the excavation of an ancient alien-insect capsule. Quatermass was battling against the Martians re-emerging. I was away at boarding school so my poor mother would watch the show every week, take notes and then send me a two-page typed summary of the programme. She did the same for my brother too!'

One of the biggest and most popular growth areas on television was sport, with an increase in the variety of sports, from football to cricket, tennis, swimming, boxing, motor racing and golf, that could be watched from home during the sixties. Viewers could get a grandstand view of the action, they could benefit from expert opinion and they could have instant replays of the highlights. For many it was a revelation – and watching sport on the box seemed almost as good as, or even better than, actually being there. As a result attendances at most sporting events went down from a high in the early fifties when top football matches regularly attracted capacity crowds of more than 50,000. One of the most popular television sports series was the BBC's

1960s FAVOURITE TELEVISION PROGRAMMES

1960: Coronation Street; Danger Man; Harry Worth; Sykes

1961: The Rag Trade; The Avengers; Morecambe and Wise Show; Songs of Praise

1962: That Was the Week That Was; The Saint; Dr Finlay's Casebook; Steptoe & Son; Z Cars; Animal Magic; University Challenge

1963: The Dick Emery Show; World In Action; Ready Steady Go; Doctor Who

1964: The Likely Lads; Top of the Pops; Crossroads; Mr and Mrs; Play School; Match of the Day; The Wednesday Play

1965: The Man from UNCLE; Jackanory; Not Only… But Also; Magic Roundabout

1966: Till Death Us Do Part; Lucky Jim; Camberwick Green; The Addams Family; Softly Softly; Star Trek; Daktari; The Frost Report; It's A Knockout; Man Alive; Skippy; Batman

1967: The Forsyte Saga; The Prisoner; Callan; Ask the Family; Captain Scarlett; Trumpton; The World This Weekend

1968: Oh Brother!; Dad's Army; Magpie; Father Dear Father; Joe 90; Basil Brush

1969: Monty Python's Flying Circus; Star Trek; The Liver Birds; Wheel of Fortune; On the Buses; Doctor in the House; the moon landing; Mary, Mungo and Midge

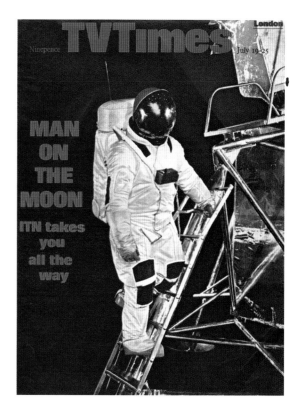

Match of the Day. It began its long Saturday night run in 1964, following England's World Cup victory that year which was watched by one of the nation's biggest ever television audiences of thirty-two million.

The popularity of television was also boosted by a number of technical innovations. The late sixties saw the beginning of colour television, which gave people a further reason to stay in with the box rather than go out to live events or the cinema. It was first introduced on BBC2 in 1967 and ITV and BBC1 followed two years later. To a public used to black-and-white television, the idea of colour was exciting and worrying. How much would the sets cost? Could the pictures capture the nuances of black and white? Initially a lot of people rented sets but many others were experimenting with their own ways of turning black-and-white into colour – by buying colour viewers, like 3-D glasses, for instance, or fitting a multicoloured plastic sheet directly over the screen for a do-it-yourself version of colour television. 'It was a layer of red, blue and green perspex. To me it was just like a sweet paper that we fitted over the telly screen. Because there were only three colours you'd always have a strip of blue sky on the top, red in the middle, and green grass on the bottom … no matter what the picture was!' recalls Elsie Murphy in Liverpool. Sports fans, in particular, welcomed the arrival of colour television: 'Now, at least you could tell which team was which!'

There were also satellites that enabled international events to be broadcast live across the world. If it was the Coronation that created the mass television audience in 1953, it was an event at the end of the sixties that once again united the viewing public. The *Apollo XI* moon landing in 1969 was billed in advance as 'the greatest show in the history of television'. Around the world 723 million people watched the fuzzy pictures of the astronauts emerging on to the moon and Neil Armstrong declaring, 'That's one small step for man, one giant leap for mankind.' John Ruthven from Flintshire was woken by his mother to watch the event. 'I didn't quite understand why she was waking me up so early in the morning but I remember going down to the living room feeling sleepy and then seeing these extraordinary pictures on the television. On the black-and-white TV the astronauts' suits were glowing white and everything else was so dark. I was gripped. Even then I knew I was witnessing history in the making.'

An unprecedented 723 million people around the world watched the *Apollo XI* moon landing, a record which stood until the Royal Wedding in 1981.

The **Car's** *the* **Star**

'IT WAS TREATED LIKE THE CROWN JEWELS. THE CAR came out just once a week on a Sunday,' remembers Dorothy Robson from her fifties childhood in Oswaldtwistle, Lancashire. 'Dad would take us all out for a spin, then wash it and put it in the garage again.' The 1950s saw the start of motoring mania in Britain. Having a car was a source of pride, a status symbol and a sign of affluence in an age of prosperity. The car – once only available to the wealthiest – came within the reach of the average family as mass-produced vehicles started to roll off production lines. Having a motor was a passport to freedom. The Sunday drive, the weekend away, the holiday, the house in the country away from the office, commuting, all became possible with an independent set of wheels. From the beginning of the fifties to the end of the sixties the number of cars on the roads increased tenfold. And novelties like the motorway, the traffic warden and the breathalyser became a familiar part of British life.

The early fifties was the final heyday of public transport, particularly the railways. The old network of thousands of lines and stations built in Victorian times had survived little changed – it was still the age of steam and most middle-class office workers commuted by rail from leafy suburbia to their offices in town. In the countryside, too, the railway was a lifeline. As well as transporting people, branch railways delivered goods between villages and even livestock went by rail. 'We were quite dependent on the Newquay–Truro line,' remembers John Harris of Cornwall. 'Some of the hamlets only had five or six little houses. If the water supply went down it was the train driver who delivered churns of water. It was a brilliant service too, you could send a basket of eggs or a few chickens two or three stations down the line. On the estate where I was working, one of the fields joined up with the main line. One of the chaps who worked with us, his wife was a wonderful cook and she would make pasties for all the men and give them to the train driver who'd slow down and drop the pasties off to us in the field.'

Towns and cities were criss-crossed by a network of trams, buses and trolleybuses. 'The trams were dead reliable,' remembers Mary Greenhough from Bradford, who went to work on one. 'Even when it was really foggy or snowing, that didn't stop them and you could hear them coming as they rattled along the tracks. The trolleybuses weren't quite as steady, you had to watch out as they were always coming off the line and the driver would have to get out and use a long pole to put it back. I remember it was smokers upstairs, so I always carried a mint with me in case I had to sit upstairs. It was a bit like an opium den. No windows open, blue with smoke.' There was a sense of camaraderie about using public transport after the war and conversations would be struck up, sometimes even friendships made. 'You seemed to meet the same people at the bus stop every morning so you'd make some comment about the weather,' says Lola Smith, who travelled to work across London by bus, 'and if you were sitting next to someone of the same age group you'd end up saying, "Well, where did you go last night?" and you'd have a chat all the way to work, and then often you'd meet the same people on the bus home and ask how their day had been.'

However, there was a mounting sense of frustration with public transport in the fifties as it often failed to get people to their exact destinations speedily. There were track problems, a legacy of the wartime bombing, on the newly nationalized railways while engines and rolling stock were in poor condition and unreliable. Buses and trams were also suffering from the ravages of the war and a long-term lack of investment. The shortcomings of the public

transport system made it particularly difficult for those who had long and complicated journeys to work – like office junior Graham Bill. 'I lived in a village in Staffordshire and my work was on the other side of Birmingham. I had to catch the 6.30 a.m. bus to Wolverhampton, then walk across to the station, catch a train from Wolverhampton to Birmingham, walk across the city centre, catch a bus to where I worked and with a bit of luck I used to get there by nine o'clock. Then there was a repeat of that journey back home, which was just about bearable in the summer months. In winter though it was a totally different story. Fog used to delay the trains and I'd get to Wolverhampton to find that the bus had gone or wasn't running because of the density of the fog, and there was nothing for it then but to walk the eight miles from Wolverhampton to Brewood. I had to walk home many, many times, sometimes when I was lucky a driver would stop and give me a lift home.' Lola Smith, too, was finding that life on the buses was starting to wear thin. 'The buses were often chock-a-block in the morning. I'd line up to get on and then it was packed, my hair might get caught in somebody's button. And there were the times when you'd wait for ages in the rain, wet and miserable, sometimes they'd be very late and then two or three would turn up at once. It was grim when it was thick fog, the buses would creep along so then you knew you were going to be late. And I'd be sitting there tense. I had to clock in at work so I'd be thinking I'm losing money here and I might even get the sack.'

One of the last trams in London on Victoria Embankment in 1952. By the early sixties trams had virtually disappeared from British cities.

Vroom, VROOM

As incomes rose it was no surprise that people wanted to have their own independent set of wheels. Since the first decades of the century the main form of private transport had been the trusty bicycle. Millions cycled as bikes were cheap, easy to repair and ideal in city traffic. Almost every family had one – and they weren't just used for work. A popular weekend or holiday activity was cycling in the countryside, sometimes on a tandem. But in the early fifties motorcycles became increasingly popular. They were relatively cheap, had many advantages over the bicycle and a man could impress a girlfriend by taking her out for a spin on his Triumph, Norton, BSA, Royal Enfield or Ariel. Once married with children, the addition of a sidecar meant the whole family could be transported long distances. Ed Mitchell from Norwich had a BSA600 Sidevalve in the early fifties. 'We'd get the four of

us on the motorbike. There was me at the front and my son Graham riding pillion, and then my wife Peggy was in the sidecar with our daughter Shirley. I never went to work on the motorbike, it was something we used for special occasions like weekends away. For the summer holidays we took the bike down to Sandy Bay near Exmouth. It took us three days to get there, with a motorbike and sidecar you couldn't do more than thirty-five or forty miles an hour. It was a pleasure to sit on the old motorbike and hear the engine throbbing beneath your legs, but Peggy wasn't so happy because the seat in the sidecar was just a bit of sponge covered over with leatherette and her bottom ached. It didn't put us off though. We went on another holiday to the Isle of Wight and that took two days to get there.' The motorbike was the main form of transport for a man and his family at the time. The popular choice amongst the younger generation was the lesser-powered motor scooter like a Vespa – its Italian manufacturers started making it under licence in Britain in 1951 – or Lambretta. Scooters were a hit amongst young professionals who wanted to dash around town, and were later adopted by mods.

The motorbike had pulling power.

BEEP *beep!*

Is it a car? Is it a motorbike? The 'bubble car' was something in between, the compromise choice for people who wanted to buy a set of wheels but didn't have money to throw about. The eccentric little three-wheeler was really no more than a motorbike with a hat on. It had no reverse gear, was economical to run and was taxed as a motorcycle. Two of the main makes were the Messerschmitt, launched in 1953 and the BMW Isetta, launched in 1962. In its short life the 'bubble car' was very popular with the young and with the married man who yearned for the feel of a motorbike but whose wife did not want to get wet. The microcars were treated as a bit of a joke when they were first launched but really came into their own during the petrol rationing that followed the Suez crisis of 1956. Jo Jones was a student when she got one. 'The bubble cars were all the rage. I had a bright yellow one. I used to drive it to college with a friend, but you had to be really careful how you sat because they were forever tipping from side to side. It broke down a lot too and there was always somebody telling me that I'd be better off walking. It was very much a free spirit, it was great, it was dry and it got you round the village and into the nearest town, but you wouldn't go on a long journey in one.'

The bubble car was a squeeze to get into – the Messerschmitt seated just two people, one behind the other tandem-style. Brian Broadhead, a driving examiner in Birmingham, found himself testing drivers in one. 'I'd have to sit behind the driver. It was very cramped and pretty frightening because you

The 'bubble car' was one step up from a motorbike and one down from a car.

couldn't reach any of the controls. There was plenty of times when I wished there'd been an ejector seat.' The car's minute size could make life awkward on a date. Alan Town bought himself a Heinkel microcar during the cold winter of 1962. 'I was really frustrated with ending up numb with cold on my motorbike. With a motorcycle licence you could buy a bubble car which meant you could wear ordinary clothes and not have to wrap up in a duffel coat to stay warm. The Heinkel had the great advantage of being able to get your passenger sitting next to you rather than behind you. I took my girlfriend on to Pangbourne Common one night, things were going well, it was getting misty inside. I remember this copper turned up and started banging on the window, saying, "Well, you can't be doing what I think you're doing in that car – it's too small." But we were! If you wanted to be a little upfront and in the warm, you could undo the seats to make it more comfortable.'

In the early fifties only 14 per cent of households had a car. It was the boss who drove – workers cycled or had motorbikes – and the idea of owning a new car was a luxury largely restricted to the well-to-do. Having one was the ultimate status symbol and the make reflected your place in the pecking order. Vauxhalls were reputed to be popular amongst doctors and Trojans

The car opened up all kinds of possibilities. Day-trips to the seaside became a reality.

were for vicars, while bank managers and accountants were often said to drive either Humbers or Armstrong-Siddeleys. Jaguars were for traders made good, Volvos for the family man and Cortinas (from 1962) were for Jack the lad types with back-seat seduction in mind. The ordinary family was likely to get one of the more inexpensive models like the Ford Anglia, Hillman Minx, Austin 7, Morris Minor or Standard 10.

Car ownership grew steadily and rapidly – by 1960 28 per cent of households had a car, 37 per cent in 1965, rising to 45 per cent in 1969. Buying a car was a great liberation – people no longer had to put up with waiting for buses or trains or suffering in bad weather. They had the freedom of the road. For Adrian Flint in Warwickshire his car changed his life. 'I was working as an apprentice confectioner cycling eight miles to work at 5 a.m. in the dark and cold. More often than not I'd get soaked and have to hang up my wet clothes on the ovens. It was my big ambition to get a car, it took me two whole years to save up for one. I never went out with a girl until I had the car. It made a huge difference, it changed my social life and gave me independence. With the car I could go out for the evening and not have to worry about getting the last bus home. It also brought me more work opportunities. My next job was fifty miles away. I couldn't have done it without the car.'

Weekends exploring more remote parts of Britain became feasible, as did day trips to the seaside and commuting longer distances to work. 'The car opened up a completely new world,' says John Harris in Cornwall. 'Previous to having a motor all I had was a boneshaker pushbike which got me around Newquay but once I acquired a car, out came the map and we were able to go places that we'd only dreamed of before. I remember going to the Chelsea Flower Show. It was about a ten-hour trip and when we got there, we had a little snooze in the car. I'll never forget this policeman who woke us up, he wanted to look at the particulars of the car, I don't think he believed that we could have come from so far away. Then there were the holidays, it was possible to go up to the Lake District and Scotland, it was like going to a foreign land. You were seeing things that you'd read about in a book. It took two or three days to get there but you could go anywhere, it was just a wonderful feeling of independence, turn the key and the engine and you were away. It was the dawn of a new era as far as I was concerned, the chance to go anywhere at any time.'

> "
> THE CAR OPENED UP A COMPLETELY NEW WORLD, PREVIOUS TO HAVING A MOTOR ALL I HAD WAS A BONESHAKER PUSHBIKE WHICH GOT ME AROUND NEWQUAY BUT ONCE I ACQUIRED A CAR, OUT CAME THE MAP AND WE WERE ABLE TO GO PLACES THAT WE'D ONLY DREAMED OF BEFORE. I REMEMBER GOING TO THE CHELSEA FLOWER SHOW. IT WAS ABOUT A TEN-HOUR TRIP AND WHEN WE GOT THERE, WE HAD A LITTLE SNOOZE IN THE CAR.
> "

OLD *Bangers*

The fifties and the sixties was the era of the old banger when a second- or third-hand car could be picked up for under fifty quid. Working-class families often made do with an old Austin or Morris that needed repairs after every long journey. Many of the vehicles were basically wrecks with floors rusted through, doors held on with string and fungus growing in the back. Pat Dallimore remembers getting a lift in one to visit her husband in hospital.

"

THE FIRST CAR I BOUGHT WAS
AN OLD AUSTIN SOMERSET. THE
SHOCK ABSORBERS WERE NON-
EXISTENT SO IT ROLLED AS IT
WENT ROUND CORNERS. AND YOU
HAD TO PUT A PINT OF OIL IN TO
EVERY TWO GALLONS OF PETROL
BECAUSE IT BURNT OIL.

"

'The car had no bottom, I could see right through to the ground. The driver turned to me and said, "It's been snowing so you better put one foot up there and the other one up the other side." So I went all the way to hospital with my legs up in the air trying to avoid the slush.'

Reg Dobson, a farmer from Warwickshire, had a succession of old bangers. 'I'd never spend more than £30 on them. One car I bought had no brakes. I remember heading for the Cheltenham races and having to look for the flattest way through the Cotswolds. No one could understand why I was going down the hills in bottom gear.' Diane Bacon in London always drove old bangers. 'The first car I bought was an old Austin Somerset. The shock absorbers were non-existent so it rolled as it went round corners. And you had to put a pint of oil in to every two gallons of petrol because it burnt oil.' Polly Carter was a devotee of old wrecks that dated from before the war. 'These old bangers had been built to last. They never went that fast and you could park them anywhere. I even learnt to drive in an old car which had no second gear. I failed the test first time, the examiner said, "You were fine except I don't understand why you never went into second gear?". One Austin 7 I had was such a leaky car it had green mould growing in the back. I'd have to stop by the side of the road to chuck the water out. For repairs I'd head down the local scrapyard with a screwdriver, hammer and wrench and spend a few hours cannibalizing extinct cars for what I needed.'

Many road accidents occurred because these ancient vehicles were poorly maintained. Faulty indicators, dodgy lights, leaks, cranky windscreen wipers and radiators boiling over were all par for the course. The days of the old banger officially came to an end in 1961 when the government introduced Ministry of Transport tests. It resulted in a huge cull and many mourned the loss of their beloved old wrecks. 'The MOTs had a big impact,'

remembers Jo Jones. 'You no longer trundled along and did your own repairs, used tights as an emergency fan belt, now it had to pass the MOT, it had to be roadworthy so you'd got to take it to a garage and pay for a mechanic to do it, which was a freedom we felt was being taken away from us. We used to drive our cars into the ground but with the MOT you could no longer do that. You had to buy another car when the repairs got to be more than the car was worth. So we got into this boring cycle of changing cars every two years, it wasn't the fun that it had been before the MOT.'

There was still a cavalier attitude to regulations and many people continued to drive their old bangers in defiance of the MOT and other rules of the road. Pat Dallimore's husband Jim used to take her out in his old Austin 7. 'He didn't have a licence, he wasn't insured, he hadn't had any driving lessons and he didn't tax the car. He wasn't bothered, but the car was in such a bad state that when we took it down to Devon on holiday Jim announced on the way back, "In no way am I going to stop this car until we get home. No stopping for the toilet because if we stop we won't be able to start again." And we went all around the back roads and no one spoke, we were all concentrating on getting home. And when he stopped outside the house and tried to start the car again, it wouldn't start, it had given up the ghost. That was the only thing that stopped us driving that car, no rules ever put us off.' Patricia Dickson, who drove a Hillman Minx in London in the sixties, remembers similarly casual attitudes to driving regulations. 'It was quite normal to drive around without insurance or tax. You'd stick a beer mat on the windscreen or leave a message in your car that you'd applied for your tax disc and that you were out at the pictures.'

The E type Jaguar was one of the flashiest cars around.

Baby, YOU CAN DRIVE MY CAR

The car had great sex appeal in the sixties. Fast driving in a luxury model – especially a sports car – was the ultimate sex symbol for a man and advertisements reinforced this image. The car became part of modern lovemaking, with sex in the back seat as part of the fantasy, and the E-Type Jaguar with its alluring lines had the sexiest image. It was launched in 1961 and its streamlined body generated the fastest speed of any production car: up to 150 m.p.h. 'If you had a flash car it attracted the girls,' recalls Alfred Roper from Derbyshire, a James Bond wannabe. 'If I ever went into town with the E-Type Jag and pulled up at a club, girls used to flock around like bees to the honey and you could pull any bird, it was all "Oh, look at that car, can I have a ride?" You'd be having a dance and chatting a bird up, she'd ask to go for a ride in the car, so I'd buy her a drink and then nip off for a spin, get up to top speed and she'd be screaming her head off. And if it was fine weather you'd get a blanket out and go into woods and enjoy yourselves, and then run her back and forget about her and get another one the next night.'

LADIES, *Start your Engines*

In 1960 only one in ten drivers were women and it tended to be the man who ruled over the family car. It was his pride and joy, something to demonstrate his status in the world and polish lovingly every Sunday. As men earned the money and bought the cars, they were reluctant to let their wives take the wheel – it was humiliating for a man to be seen being driven by his wife. However, when the sixties sexual revolution got into full swing women, too, wanted to get behind the wheel. They were going out to work, they needed their own cars and, because they had their own incomes, they could afford them. But motoring was one of the areas in which sexism lingered. Driving was a man's world and jokes abounded about the incompetence of women drivers even though, statistically, they drove more safely than men. 'Men were very condescending, they always thought that no woman could ever drive as well as they could and if you dared to overtake them or beat one of them at the lights they would do everything to overtake you or get back at you,' remembers Diane Bacon, who took to the roads in London. Christine Fagg remembers one telling incident in her driving life. 'It was a Friday evening and I was in the car in the driveway about to leave for the weekend when a friend of my husband's pulled up, waved to say

The Morris Mini Minor in 1962. Driving was a man's world but women wanted their share of the action.

GREAT
LITTLE CARS

QUALITY FIRST

MORRIS

hello and then parked his car across the driveway and went in to talk to Graham. Well, I sat there fuming with the car blocked, slowly coming to boiling point. Ten minutes later Bob was still inside talking to Graham and, now steaming, I went inside and told Bob that I really needed to get on my way and could he move his car which was blocking the drive. Bob was amazed. "You're taking the car out on your own? Well, I've heard of women's lib, but a woman driving off on her own, now that's ridiculous." And he was absolutely serious.' Some women, like Patricia Dickson, turned the sexism to their advantage and played the innocent. 'If I was having trouble with the car, I'd smile sweetly and there was always some man who'd come along and say, "I'll help you out, you silly old thing, leave it to me." Or I'd go out on a date with an empty tank and the man would say, "Oh dear, I'd better put some petrol into your car, hadn't I?" They loved coming to the rescue and I didn't mind either.'

The first car to be marketed for the independent woman was the Mini. Launched in 1959, it was the motoring icon of the Swinging Sixties. It was young, hip and revolutionary, just like the decade, and was driven by the fashionable from lords and ladies to labourers. Sixties stars like the Beatles, Mick Jagger, Twiggy, Peter Sellers and Lord Snowdon were seen buzzing around London, taking advantage of its compact size which made it easy to park in the capital's crowded streets. It even landed a part in the movies,

Britain fell in love with the Mini. There was even a craze for customizing them to make the car more personal.

featuring as Michael Caine's getaway car in *The Italian Job*. The original Mini was designed by Sir Alec Issigonis from a doodle on a cigarette packet when he was asked to produce a small, economical car to cope with the effects of petrol rationing after the Suez crisis. Right from the start it was clear that Issigonis, who had previously designed the Morris Minor, had created something that redefined the small car. Previously no one had conceived of the engine and gearbox sharing the same oil, something that helped to make the layout more compact. The Mini, though more than 2 feet shorter than the Minor, had the same amount of room inside and could hold four people. The first Mini to roll off the production lines of the British Motor Corporation in 1959 cost £469.

Polly Carter was young, newly engaged and working in Swinging London when she bought her first Mini in 1964. 'It was nippy, it was zippy, brand new, went like stink and no danger of electrocution like the old bangers I'd driven before. It was just fantastic to have an efficient car where there was no need to carry a roll of newspaper to mop up leaks. We got everything into that car. We even moved house with it. I always had Minis after that, white ones so you couldn't see the dirt on them. If you saw another Mini coming towards you, you'd toot your horn and wave at the other car. It was like being in a club. They epitomized the young feeling of the time, they were enormous fun.' The nation fell in love with the Mini and bought them by the thousand. There was even a craze for customizing them by adding personal touches. The cars were painted psychedelic colours, festooned with flowers, pop stars turned them into limousines and hatchbacks, the hub caps were removed and wheel spacers put on. The Mini's status as the dynamic car of the times was confirmed when a souped-up version won the Monte Carlo Rally three times in a row, in 1964, 1965 and 1967.

By the late sixties the amount of cars on the road was reaching an all-time high. The number of owners doubled during the decade from 5.6 million to 11.8 million. The love affair with the car had a devastating effect on public transport – trams and cars competed for road space and it was the car that won. Virtually all the tramlines in Britain had disappeared by the early sixties, with Glasgow the last major city to lose hers in 1962. Trolleybuses went on running until the late sixties. In particular, the shift from rail to road had

> "
> IT WAS NIPPY, IT WAS ZIPPY, BRAND NEW, WENT LIKE STINK AND NO DANGER OF ELECTROCUTION LIKE THE OLD BANGERS I'D DRIVEN BEFORE. IT WAS JUST FANTASTIC TO HAVE AN EFFICIENT CAR WHERE THERE WAS NO NEED TO CARRY A ROLL OF NEWSPAPER TO MOP UP LEAKS. WE GOT EVERYTHING INTO THAT CAR. WE EVEN MOVED HOUSE WITH IT. I ALWAYS HAD MINIS AFTER THAT. IT WAS LIKE BEING IN A CLUB. IF YOU SAW ANOTHER MINI COMING TOWARDS YOU, YOU'D TOOT YOUR HORN.
> "

wide-ranging and devastating consequences. In 1963 Dr Richard Beeching of British Railways announced a plan for extensive cuts to deal with the huge losses the railways were sustaining and nearly a third of the rail network was closed down, with the loss of 2128 stations and nearly 70,000 jobs. It was the end of passenger trains in most parts of north and central Wales, the West Country and north of Inverness in Scotland. It was a catastrophe for the rural communities who lost their lifeline and many people found themselves without a viable form of transport and were thus coerced into buying a car or moving house.

More cars on the road meant more congestion, and better controls were needed to keep the traffic moving. New measures included one-way systems, prohibited right turns and urban clearways. Push-button controls were introduced at panda crossings for pedestrians in 1962 and a fifty miles an hour speed limit on all trunk roads was imposed in 1965. The planners also managed to give birth to one of the most unpopular jobs in Britain when, in 1960, they unleashed the first traffic wardens on to Mayfair in

Just the ticket. Traffic wardens first patrolled the streets of London in 1960.

London. 'It was annoying because we'd had free rein on the roads up to then, apart from police officers who would stop you occasionally,' remembers Terry Shanahan. 'But suddenly these traffic wardens were all over the streets in the West End, and they brought out painted areas which were parking bays with a meter and you put sixpence in it for two hours of parking. But no way were we going to pay for parking on the streets. We saw traffic wardens as a blight because they were there to stop us doing the things we wanted to do. The first thing they brought out were the yellow lines, then they started getting heavy with these marks on the kerb which no one understood. So these wardens used to come along and put this thing on your windscreen which we'd pull off and screw up and throw at them, and they used to shout and threaten you with prosecution and stand there defying you to move while they put this thing back on your windscreen. No doubt about it, the warden was the enemy of the people, they were primarily older men, they looked to us like they were ex-servicemen, probably a sergeant or a horrible little corporal from somewhere.'

'DON'T DRINK *and* DRIVE'

Drink-driving simply wasn't seen as a sin in the sixties and most people didn't think twice about returning home sozzled after a night out. 'It wasn't a big deal then,' says Ken Hedges. 'We'd drive back from the pub with three in the back and two in the boot with their legs dangling over the edge.' Reg Dobson had a similar attitude. 'I would go and play darts in Rugby and down a couple of bottles of beer. One night I smacked into a tree on the way home and a copper happened to be on the other side of the road and came over to see if I was all right. He wasn't bothered by the fact I'd downed a few. People

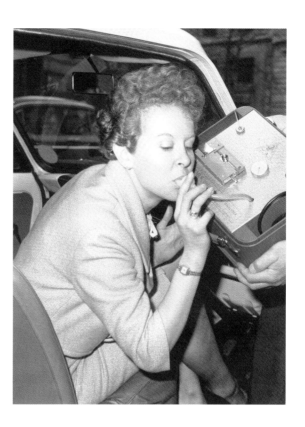

Over the limit? The Drink-Meter was an early form of breathalyser.

didn't mind so much about drink-driving then and there were fewer cars on the road anyhow.' Diane Bacon remembers one incident that went too far even for the then-casual approach to drinking and driving. 'I used to have a drink and drive, but before I got in the car I always made sure I could walk in a straight line because that was the test in those days. Well, I was really drunk one night, and I am forever disgusted by this, but I actually got someone to put the key in the ignition because I couldn't quite manage it. It was only a short distance home but thankfully I only did it the once.'

However, accidents were on the increase with nearly 8000 deaths on the road in 1966, the worst year ever for fatalities. Public information films encouraged people to develop good driving practices and avoid the example of Reginald Molehusband, the fictional character who couldn't park his car. 1967 was the watershed year during which the government introduced a raft of regulations to tackle the growing problems of the road. The most significant measure was the introduction of the breathalyser test. Until then there had been no specific drink-driving legislation and a policeman's powers to stop a motorist who was driving while drunk were no greater than those he had to stop a pedestrian who was drunk and disorderly. The most sophisticated test he could carry out was to smell the driver's breath or ask him to walk in a straight line. In the same year, seat belts were made compulsory in new cars, the 70 m.p.h. speed limit was introduced and all cars more than three years old had to take an annual MOT – the test introduced in 1961 had applied only to cars more than ten years old.

The number of accidents fell immediately after the introduction of these regulations, with deaths on the roads dropping by a quarter within a few months of the arrival of the breathalyser test. Motorists, however, grumbled – they viewed the restrictions as a loss of personal freedom. Polly Carter was one such disgruntled driver. 'There were limits on the roads but somehow road signs didn't mean an awful lot. We weren't as law-abiding as now, we really thought it was an infringement on our privacy. I remember safety belts coming in and I thought they were dreadful. I didn't wear mine for ages, in fact people even knitted sweaters with a safety belt in them so that it looked like they already had a seat belt on when they were sat in their cars. It was Big Brother as far as I was concerned, somebody telling me that I had to wear a seat belt.'

The MOTORWAY

Motorways were the ultimate symbol of modern motoring and an ambitious programme to build them got under way in the late fifties. The original vision was linked to a wartime ideal of a modern Britain with fast roads free from pedestrians and bicycles, the need for which was made more urgent by the appalling traffic congestion that had resulted from the huge rise in car-ownership. The first stretch to open was eight miles of the M6 near Preston in 1958. Dorothy Robson lived nearby. 'I used to get on to my brother's bike and cycle up to the bridge over the motorway and gawp at the cars going by. There weren't that many cars on it at the time, it seemed like something out of the future.' The M1 opened in 1959. Fred Fisher from Suffolk remembers driving on it for the first time. 'We were away for the weekend visiting relatives and I decided to take the family for a spin on the M1. Well, it was absolutely terrifying seeing the cars go by at such speed. I stuck to the slow lane, I didn't have the nerve to go into the middle lane to overtake. In any case the old car would probably have packed up if I'd nudged the speed up.' The motorway network allowed people to go further for weekend treats and holidays. For Winifred Hughes, it made all the difference to her holidays. 'We were living in the Midlands then and taking our holidays in Weston-super-Mare. Before the motorway it would take all day to get down to the seaside. We'd get up in the middle of the night, pack sandwiches and a flask and start the drive down which would take most of the day. Once the M5 was built we could do it in a few hours and the motorways were pretty empty then too.' Even going to a motorway service station was seen as the hip, new thing to do. As a teenager Dorothy Robson would head for the services on the M6. 'The service station stayed open late, so we used to make a special trip there after a night out and feast on burger and chips. Perfect.'

By 1969 600 miles of motorway had been built, cementing the foundations of the network. The car had more of an impact on the way we run our lives than any other comparable modern invention, and the massive programme of road-building had transformed the landscape of city and countryside alike. There was no going back. Modern Britain had become a nation of car-owners.

Motorway rescue on the M74 in 1968. The RAC first introduced roadside emergency telephone boxes in 1912.

chapter

The **Sexual** *revolution*

THE SIXTIES HAVE GONE DOWN IN NATIONAL folklore as the decade of the sexual revolution. What had once been a private act became a public obsession. Sex became the ultimate personal pleasure and individuals demanded the right to fulfilment inside and outside of marriage. With the coming of the Pill, there was a blossoming of sexual freedom and experimentation amongst young people. For some, sex became a political act – open relationships, sex before marriage and group sex all seemed like a blow against bourgeois morality. Many older people, alarmed at what they saw as a collapse of personal morality and discipline, harked back to the fifties as a golden age of marital bliss and sexual fulfilment. This is the story of the profound sexual changes in Britain during the fifties and sixties. To tell it we draw mainly on the personal experience of our interviewees.

Previous page The last dance in 1957. The fifties and sixties saw a revolution in young people's sexual attitudes.

ittle is known of the intimate lives of the British during these two decades. There were a few sex surveys yet, as always, they only scratched the surface. Landmark sixties events like the *Lady Chatterley* censorship trial and the Profumo affair were widely discussed, but the sex lives of ordinary men and women have remained largely a mystery. Their stories help to shed some light on one of the most dramatic eras of sexual change in twentieth-century history.

Virgin BRIDES

When the fifties began Victorian sexual values remained a potent force in British society. Early sex surveys showed that the majority of people still believed in the ideal of the virgin bride, and the Church remained influential in preaching the sanctity of marriage and the sin of 'fornication'. So, too, did parents of all social classes. Romances were still closely vetted by both sets of parents, often over Sunday tea, to make sure a match was suitable. The virginity of a daughter was widely regarded as a prized asset in the marriage market and courtship involved the observance of a ritual of female innocence and chastity. She should behave like a 'young lady' and he should behave like a 'young gentleman'. Crucially, this involved sexual abstinence.

Back yard lovers in 1952. When young fifties couples succumbed to the temptations of sex it usually took place in back alleys, parks and fields.

It was accepted that a young man had strong urges and if he failed to contain them – as was thought to be natural from time to time – it was the duty of the young lady to resist. 'I nearly lost my honour several times when I was courting Vic,' remembers Jo Roffey from south London. 'It wasn't for lack of trying on his part that we didn't do it. It was never say die. Whether we were in the pictures or if he was walking me home, he'd try and get his old boy out, he even did it once in the front room when my mum had gone out to make a cup of tea. I never did it though, you just didn't then. I wanted to save myself for my wedding night. If my dad had found we'd done anything he'd have killed me, I was terrified of him.'

Shotgun WEDDINGS

However, many young couples did succumb to the temptation of sex before marriage. It was usually rushed. They did it against walls in back alleys – the 'knee trembler' – on overcoats in the park, in fields and on sofas when parents had gone out to the pictures or to the shops. Sexual ignorance and not using contraceptives meant many girls had no protection against pregnancy – and once a young woman was pregnant a marriage was usually hastily arranged to avoid any scandal. Between a quarter and a third of all marriages in the early fifties were shotgun weddings. 'I had a forced marriage,' says Renee Davidson from Wakefield. 'I was so upset. I didn't want to do it. We went for a walk in the country and he forced himself on me. I couldn't believe I was pregnant. We used the withdrawal method, I didn't really understand it then but he obviously didn't withdraw in time. It spoilt it for me because everybody knew where we lived that we had to get married. And you couldn't get married in church, they wouldn't let you, it had to be in a register office and I'd so looked forward to having a proper white wedding.'

'Fallen WOMEN'

The gossip and blame was generally directed towards the 'fallen woman' and the unmarried mother had to face the stigma of her child's illegitimacy, which still remained strong in the post-war years. Although the more fortunate girls were looked after by their parents, many were driven from their homes, lost their jobs and had to seek refuge in mother and baby homes which were usually run by the Church. The treatment they received was harsh and humiliating and their babies were normally removed for adoption. This was the fate of around 40,000 young women every year. But not all submitted meekly to these punitive regimes and gave up their babies. 'I got pregnant the first time I had sex, I was an innocent,' remembers Dot Stephenson from Hull. 'My boyfriend was in the army, I met him at a dance and we'd been going out for about two months when we committed the dreadful act as it was called then and I fell for a baby. We'd been drinking, I didn't like it, I didn't enjoy it, to me it was nothing, but unfortunately I got pregnant. I daren't tell my parents and by the time I was certain I was expecting he'd been posted to Scotland. I decided the only thing I could do was to find him so I hitch-hiked all the way there. I couldn't find him so I ended up in a Church of England mother and baby home. They treated you abominably, you were treated like bad girls. It was all washing floors and polishing and cleaning and going to church. They even made me clean and polish the parquet flooring with a toothbrush. When I'd had the baby they went to take him away and told me he was being adopted. I said, "You're not adopting him, I haven't agreed to that." The sister was pulling him away from me. Well I gave her one heave, I punched her so hard my fist went through this glass window, so I picked up the baby, the blood was pouring out of my hand and we were both covered in blood and I ran away. They called the police in and tracked me down, but my mum put her foot down and supported me, she helped me keep the baby and look after him.'

HONEYMOON *Hiccups*

Couples who had played it safe and refrained from sex before marriage could have their problems, too. The romantic climax of the wedding night was sometimes a disaster as neither partner knew what to do. Jo Roffey married at the age of eighteen in 1958. 'I had a lovely little baby-doll nightie on, a short frilly thing. Well, I didn't have it on for long, as soon as we got into bed it came off. But when it came to sex I didn't know what to do. Vic got cross and started shouting at me saying I'd got the rhythm all wrong. We couldn't do it.

I regretted getting married, I thought sod this, I want to go home.' Vic Roffey remembers, 'I was so excited, I'd been waiting so long, Jo was so lovely and although I'd had sex before I was very nervous about doing it with her. I'd had too much to drink and it was partly a case of brewer's droop. I started telling her off then, blaming her, it was right out of order.'

Some distressed newly-weds sought medical help after returning from their honeymoons. 'We went to Paris after our wedding,' says Anne Grundy from Worthing, who was married in 1957. 'It hurt so much when my husband made love to me the first time, there was blood on the sheets. I thought that it must have been because I was a virgin and it would get better. It didn't. The sex was a disaster and I kept making excuses not to do it. When we came home I saw my mother and burst into floods of tears, I was so miserable, I said, "I can't have sex." She got me to see a specialist in Harley Street, an elderly man, and he undressed me, then he produced a case. And I know this sounds odd but inside it were plastic penises of all shapes and sizes and he said, "About what size is your husband's?" I hadn't a clue, I was so embarrassed I just pointed to the nearest one. Then he took it out and he started arousing me. There was a nurse there, it was all above board. I started to fancy him and when he put it up I didn't want him to take it out, it was so nice. Then he stopped and he said, "There's nothing wrong with you, you just need to tell your husband to touch you and arouse you before he makes love, then it won't hurt." That's what I did and it was certainly much

A bar scene in 1958. The great fear associated with sex before marriage in the pre-Pill days was an unwanted pregnancy.

171

better after that. In fact, my husband enjoyed it so much he started wanting sex twice a night. I just couldn't keep up with it, I was exhausted because I had to get up early and go to work every morning.'

In a few cases the bride associated sex and sin so profoundly that it was some time before she could begin a sexual relationship with her husband. Some developed vaginismus, a clamping of the vagina due to anxiety and fear, that made penetrative sex impossible. Eva Moffat from Manchester was married in 1956. 'I'd got so used to stopping him from making love to me and saying it was wrong, that when we were married and it was right, it still seemed all wrong to me. It went on for several months after we were married. When my husband came near me to have sex I tensed up so much we couldn't do anything. I used to have my head pressed up against the end of the bed and he'd try everything, he was so patient, but it was useless. Eventually when we did do it I got pregnant more or less straightaway and after that it was all right.'

A bride and groom pictured in 1960. The romantic climax of many a marriage was still spoiled by sexual ignorance.

A few marriages remained unconsummated, one of the problems dealt with by Rose Hacker, a marriage guidance counsellor in London in the fifties and sixties. 'People don't realize how many unconsummated marriages there were then. Impotence was the main problem, it was almost always psychological, a result of early training, guilt or fear. Sometimes a man had been active with prostitutes, women he despised, so that with a woman he admired and loved, he just couldn't do these dirty things. That split was still quite common. He worshipped his wife, she was like the Virgin Mary, but he couldn't possibly have sex with her. It's amazing how many people put up with these sexless marriages. The longest one I had was twenty-five years.'

Lavender MARRIAGE

Amongst the unconsummated marriages of the fifties were those in which one of the partners was gay or lesbian. In a decade before gay rights were established, and when there was immense hostility to homosexuals, men and women who were uncertain and confused about their sexuality found themselves pressurized into marriage. One of them was Cambridge graduate Noel Currer-Briggs, the eldest son of a wealthy middle-class family from Yorkshire. 'At Cambridge I fell in love with a girl I'd known as a boy. It was an intellectual love rather than a physical love, we had a lot in common. I was very family conscious, I was the eldest son and I felt it was my duty to get married and produce children. I asked her to marry me and she accepted. But before we married I went to see a doctor to ask his advice. I was a virgin and I was rather worried that I had fantasies about men not women. He reassured me and said, "Well if you're not an artist and you're not effeminate you can't be homosexual." The honeymoon was ghastly. Both of us were virgins and I just couldn't do it. I wasn't aroused by her at all. It carried on for several years, we ran a farm in Gloucestershire and I was tired with work so it was never a big issue and we never spoke about it. Until one day I decided to see another doctor and he told me I was gay. When I told my wife she burst into tears and asked if she'd done something wrong. It was far tougher on her than me. She wanted us to stay together and we remained married for the next fifteen years. In the meantime I got a job in London and spent the week there living an entirely gay life.'

A lovers' picnic on Wimbledon common in 1957. During the fifties and sixties there was a shift away from the sexual puritanism of the past.

GOOD *Sex* GUIDE

In the fifties a good sex life was regarded as essential to a strong and healthy marriage, an important source of pleasure. This represented a big shift in attitudes since the first decades of the century when sexual puritanism deemed that the main justification for sex was procreation. Since the 1920s feminist birth-control campaigners like Marie Stopes had advocated more effective methods of contraception so that sex could be enjoyed without the constant fear of an unwanted pregnancy. They also argued that the wife's right to sexual fulfilment was as vital as that of her husband. Pioneering inter-war doctors like Helena Wright taught married women how to achieve orgasm by stimulating their clitoris. By the 1950s education by the birth control and marriage guidance movements had helped many married couples to avoid the sexual ignorance and fear that had blighted sex lives in the past. However, there was a new trend in the fifties which again geared sex towards male pleasure. The current literature stressed the importance of regular lovemaking two or three times a week or more in order to satisfy the powerful male sex drive. According to Freud – whose theories were now shaping modern attitudes to sex – this was essential for a man's physical and mental health. This was very different to the advice given thirty years earlier by Marie Stopes in her best-selling *Married Love*, in which she had emphasized that lovemaking should be attuned to the rhythms of a woman's body, which might mean weeks of abstinence followed by short bursts of passionate sex. The advice some marriage guidance counsellors gave to wives who were tired of regular, timetabled sex was that it was their duty to satisfy their man. It was all part of being a modern, glamorous and superefficient housewife. A woman who didn't enjoy regular sex risked being labelled frigid. 'My husband wanted sex every night and it was too much for me,' remembers Janet Hill from Liverpool. 'I was tired out after a long day's work and looking after the children. It wasn't enjoyable for me at all. But the advice I got was that the problem was mine and that really I should just do it and pretend to enjoy it or he'd look for it elsewhere.'

Conjugal RIGHTS

This was a variation on the theme of the man's conjugal rights, which had long been the justification for a husband's desire for sex on demand. This fundamental right, backed by the law and the man's physical force, was still basic to the sex lives of many married couples. It was especially strong amongst working-class men, and their wives had sex out of a sense of duty. Early surveys – and couples' memories – suggest that it was almost always initiated by the husband. There was little or no foreplay and generally only one position: the missionary position. It was all over quickly, often within one or two, or at most, five minutes – sex finished when the man experienced orgasm. Many women got little or no pleasure from it and few enjoyed regular orgasms. A good husband was regarded as one who was not too sexually demanding and who didn't use violence to get his way. 'I wasn't one of the lucky ones,' says Renee Lester, a mother of six from Scunthorpe. 'Every night I'd maybe read for a bit and keep my eye ready on the clock for when he came home from the pub. He'd be home around ten to eleven. When I heard footsteps I'd blow the lamp out and pretend to be asleep. He would come home full of romance and full of beer and start mauling me. I just wanted to sleep and it used to cause no end of trouble if I refused him. You'd get a swipe if you didn't. And sometimes they'd say, "Oh bugger you if that's the way you feel." I didn't care if he said that, but mostly they demanded their rights. There was no affection with it, no love, they just wanted sex. It was a duty, a horrible duty to me, I didn't like it. A woman didn't get satisfaction from sex then, she was just disgusted with it, if

> **"**
> MY WIFE WOULD PRETEND THAT SHE'D HEARD THE BABY CRYING. I'D NEVER HEARD HIM BUT SHE'D BRING HIM IN AND PUT HIM BETWEEN US. THAT WAS LIKE A 6-INCH WALL WITH BARBED WIRE ON IT, HE WAS THERE BECAUSE SHE DIDN'T WANT SEX. WHEN SHE'D DONE THAT TWO OR THREE TIMES I THOUGHT, "AYE, THAT'S HER FAVOURITE PLOY NOW," THAT MEANT THERE'S NOWT DOWN FOR YOU CHARLIE.'
> **"**

she was owt like me. And you'd lie there and you'd be looking at the cracks in the ceiling thinking, "Oh that crack could do with filling in, that could do with a bit of whitewashing." It was no fun, it was just nasty, dirty and degrading.'

The husband's sexual power was rooted in his economic domination of the marriage. Ray Rochford was a young father who worked in the building trade in Salford in the fifties. 'You were the lord and master in those days. You were the main breadwinner, most women didn't work then. It was the man's wages that ran the house and you took advantage of that fact. I would expect sex when I wanted it, when I felt like it, whether she'd worked hard all day, whether the kids had been difficult, it made no difference to me, I wanted sex so I had it. And my wife would think, "Oh best get it over with," because to them sex was a thing apart, but to a man it was everything, it was that era you see. It's very sad looking back because they'd often make up any excuse to get out of it. My wife would pretend that she'd heard the baby crying. I'd never heard him but she'd bring him in and put him between us. That was like a 6-inch wall with barbed wire on it, he was there because she didn't want sex. When she'd done that two or three times I thought, "Aye, that's her favourite ploy now," that meant there's nowt down for you Charlie.'

Faking IT

For many women sex became another chore to add to their domestic duties. Some would make a pretence of sexual pleasure or orgasm to make their husband climax more quickly – faking it long predated *When Harry Met Sally*. 'I used to count up how many times I'd had sex that week and if I hadn't had it for a time I'd be there doing my housework thinking, God I'll probably have to do it tonight,' remembers Helen Hackney from Chester. 'I often didn't feel like it, and there'd be rows about it if I said no because he thought it was his right. So what I'd do was to fake an orgasm, do all the oohs and aahs. I discovered that doing that made him come that much quickly, it would all be over in a minute.'

Other women faked orgasm to boost their husband's ego and make sure he didn't stray outside the marriage looking for sexual excitement. But for Jo Roffey this led to an unexpected problem. 'I would always fake it, I wouldn't let on that I wasn't getting anything from the sex or he'd go and get it somewhere else. That went on for six years and I kept making all the right noises, but on one Sunday afternoon, the kids were playing downstairs, I actually reached an orgasm. I thought it was so amazing, marvellous, but it was a shame because I wasn't able to share it with Vic because he thought I'd been reaching them since day one. So he was none the wiser. But after that day I never looked back, we were doing it all the time, the sex was wonderful.'

For some couples lovemaking got better as they became more sexually confident and experienced after several years of marriage. Greater affluence and better housing conditions also improved their sex lives – there was more privacy, a warm bedroom and a bathroom to wash in afterwards. 'It got so much better,' remembers Joyce Tucker from Exeter. 'When we were sharing a room with my daughter we could only do it when she was asleep and we were terrified of waking her up, so you had to be very quiet. After we moved and we had our own bedroom with central heating it was wonderful. We could do it whenever we wanted and make as much noise as we wanted. And with a nice indoor bathroom too, that meant I had somewhere to wash and keep the cap that I'd got from the clinic.'

The PILL

What changed the sex lives of the British more than anything else, however, was the advent of the contraceptive pill. It went on sale in 1961 and for the first time in history women had a virtually foolproof defence against unwanted pregnancies. It was easy to use, it was regarded as being completely safe and it was available on the National Health. To begin with it was only prescribed to married women. The take-up rate was phenomenal – by 1964 half a million were taking the Pill and the birth rate was falling. The danger of pregnancy had been a constant fear in the past,

> The contraceptive pill which first went on sale in 1961 lay behind the sixties' sexual revolution. For the first time in history women had a virtually foolproof defence against unwanted pregnancy.

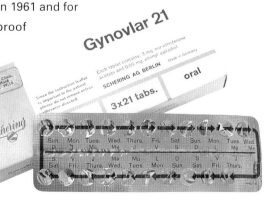

reducing sexual pleasure for many couples. Despite the baby boom of the post-war years, most people still wanted to restrict the size of their family to two or three children but before the Pill there had been no really safe and effective method of contraception. Rubber condoms had improved since before the war but were still unpopular because they desensitized the sex act and were notoriously unreliable. A small minority of women used the cap, recommended by birth control clinics, but these could be messy and were time-consuming to put in and take out. Most couples used the withdrawal method, the most dangerous form of contraception as many men failed to withdraw in time, and after a few disasters that resulted in unplanned pregnancies many people used partial abstinence to avoid having more babies. 'That was the only safe thing to do, not to do it,' remembers Joyce Mitchell from Stoke-on-Trent. 'After we'd been caught out once with our daughter, we'd go weeks without doing it. The fewer times you did it, the less chance there was of having another. You didn't really understand what was the safe period then. It could be very frustrating, especially for my husband, but he was a patient man and he didn't want any more children either.' With the coming of the Pill all these fears vanished and sex could now be enjoyed in a more carefree and spontaneous way. 'When I went on the Pill it was fantastic, we could do it whenever we wanted,' says Joyce. 'I enjoyed it more because I was so relaxed.'

Sexual LIBERATION

But the biggest impact of the Pill was to encourage sex outside marriage. Young women, now able to control their fertility for the first time, started to abandon the old sexual mores that stigmatized the sexually active single girl. This rejection of conventional sexuality had begun in the pre-Pill days of the fifties when beatnik students proclaimed the right of young people to have sex before marriage. Although many young people had defied this taboo in the past, doing so had generally been secretive – and, even amongst the more liberal, lovemaking was usually only regarded as acceptable between long-term partners who planned to get married. Now beatniks, believing that nuclear warfare would soon bring the world to an end, decided to live for the moment and enjoy sex before it was too late. 'To be a beatnik in Tunbridge Wells was thought terribly shocking,' says Caroline Wilson. 'I rejected a lot of what I'd been brought up to hold dear. I wore bohemian clothes, I hung out on Brighton beach, we begged and we busked. But what was most shocking of all for my parents were the beatnik ideas about free love. For us free love meant we believed in sex before marriage, nothing more than that. To my mother though that was so terrible. She told me that if I did it nobody would want to marry me, I'd be tainted for ever. A woman who had sex before marriage to her was disreputable and hopeless and dreadful, a kind of fallen woman. She said that she'd be able to tell when I'd done it, it would show on my face and I wouldn't be welcome at home any more because I'd be a bad influence on my little stepbrother and sister. They were only aged about two or three. So it was a big step away from everything I'd been brought up to when I did it. And I was terrified. I lost my virginity to Jesus John, so-called because of his big beard, he was quite a famous beatnik in the south of England. We went out together for about nine months and I did it for love. I wondered if my mother would be able to tell when I went home after we'd done it, but of course she couldn't.'

Teenagers kiss and dance the night away at an all-night carnival of jazz, at London's Albert Hall in 1959. The rejection of conventional sexuality had begun in the pre-Pill days.

At first it was very difficult for single girls to get the Pill. Family planning clinics refused to give it to anyone who was unmarried and most GPs were reluctant to prescribe it for them. It was not until Helen Brook, a banker's wife who had for years been involved in family planning work, established the Brook clinics in 1964 that single girls had easy access to the contraceptive pill. The clinics were an attempt to help young women avoid the distress of unwanted pregnancies. Abortion was not legalized until 1967 and before then as many as thirty-five to forty women died each year from criminal backstreet abortions. To begin with, all the single women who were seen by the Brook clinics were given psychiatric counselling before contraception was prescribed. The demand for the Pill amongst young women was huge and in the second half of the sixties attitudes towards it changed dramatically. By the end of the decade most GPs and family planning clinics were prescribing it and almost a half of all women in their early twenties were on the Pill.

Swinging SIXTIES

The years between 1965 and 1969 were when the sexual revolution began in Britain. The pace of change was astonishing – and the Pill made it all possible. This was the beginning of recreational sex for young women as well as young men. Single men had always wanted to sow their wild oats but there had been a shortage of willing partners. The girl's role had been to domesticate the man's sexual instincts by withholding sex until she was engaged or married. This changed as the new hedonistic movement gathered strength amongst young middle-class women. The late sixties was the period when Swinging London was at the forefront of the sexual changes, the powerhouse of the sexually permissive movement. It set the trend and attracted rebellious teenage girls eager to break with convention and have fun. Many, like Biba twin Rosie Young, were on the Pill. 'It was wonderful to go on the Pill, it was easy to get and it gave you a marvellous sense of freedom. It made it possible to be promiscuous. That's what we wanted to be. I had lots of casual sexual relationships and even with one-night stands I'd often go back and sleep with a man. I wasn't looking for love or Mr Right, I just wanted to have fun. It was a whole different way of looking at sex and having sex and not worrying about the consequences. Working in Biba's I was getting invites to all the clubs and the parties and I was mixing with photographers and fashion designers and club-owners. It was a great adrenalin rush to be at the heart of the scene. A man might come up to me and say, "Fly to Nice with me for the weekend." You knew that sleeping with him was part of the deal, you weren't going to be in separate rooms and that could be great fun. Then a few days later you might go to a club, get a bit drunk, smoke a bit of dope and end up sleeping with someone else. It was great to be young and attractive and to be going out with other young and attractive people. Sometimes you'd get the odd infection, then you'd pop off down to St George's VD clinic, get another pill and that sorted you out. No, I was happy, it was a great time to be young and it seemed that anything was possible.'

Amongst the trailblazers of the sexual revolution were sixth-form girls and young women at university who also began to go on the Pill in large numbers. They wanted to be part of the rebellious youth culture that was flowering in the Swinging Sixties. And as the counterculture developed in the 1967 Summer of Love, being sexually active was a political act, a rejection of narrow bourgeois values – the institution of marriage itself seemed under threat. But changing the world through free sex wasn't as simple as it seemed. One of the sixth-formers who went on the Pill around this time was Linda Shanovitch from north London. 'The sixties were such an exciting time to be a teenager, it was all new and exciting, all the music and the fashion, all the songs were about love and sex and you just wanted to be a part of that. I went on the Pill when I was sixteen. I just went to my GP and said I was having sex and I needed some contraception. Actually I hadn't had sex by then but I intended to soon. I was a sixth-former living at home and if my parents had known they would have been horrified and thrown me out, so I didn't tell them. The Pill made sex completely free of any anxiety about having babies, so in a way we

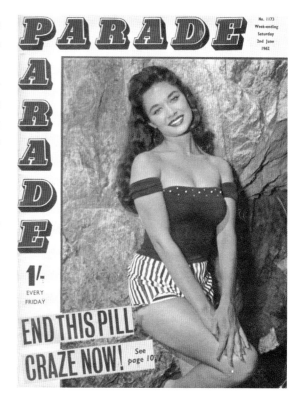

The Pill made recreational sex possible for young women as well as young men. The institution of marriage itself seemed under threat.

became like men, we could have sex without worrying about the consequences. So I went round hunting for some way of losing my virginity, it was something I had to get rid of before I could start enjoying life. I did it with a boy on a piece of wasteground and I was inoculated against my virginity. It was nothing, not enjoyable, but I wasn't going to be easily defeated. I fell in love with my art teacher, he seemed the pinnacle of all carnal knowledge. I stayed on after a party at his place and that was the beginning of a relationship that lasted seven years. We did everything. He got me into free love. I wanted to believe in it, you wanted to make the world a better place, create a world where people didn't own each other, they weren't jealous, they weren't possessive. I thought I'm strong enough to do this, to share my wonderful man with my wonderful friends. He wanted me to have group sex and I did that too. We were breaking all the taboos, so we thought. But we had our own taboos and one of them was we couldn't talk about our problems or admit to being unhappy. I'm quite shocked looking back how unfulfilled I was. It was exciting to begin with but the sex was not really enjoyable. I rarely had an orgasm, because the men were so selfish. And I didn't feel loved in the way I wanted to be. We were in love with the sixties and we just didn't have the confidence to say, "No, that's not right, I don't want to do that." That comes with age, but I certainly learnt a lot.'

Teenage SEX

The trend was for young people to have sex at an earlier age. And by the late sixties the influence of the new sex, drugs and rock 'n' roll culture was seeping downwards to reach ever-younger teenagers. Many of them were from well-to-do backgrounds – working-class girls tended to be more sexually conservative, fearing the stigma of a bad reputation and the taunts of 'slag' or 'slut' – and increasing numbers of middle-class girls as young as thirteen or fourteen were sexually active and on the Pill. 'My mum put me on the Pill when I was fourteen,' says Lorraine West from St Albans. 'I was a wild child, I was having sex, I was smoking dope, I was dropping acid, I thought I knew it all. I wanted to break free from my background, the private school and boring suburbia. I wanted to shock. I wore the most outrageous clothes, I had a star on my forehead, I had Alice Cooper eyelashes and I listened to Jimi

Hendrix very loud in my bedroom with boys jumping in and out of the windows all the time – luckily it was a bungalow. My school couldn't control me and I was expelled when I was fourteen. I ran off to join a free-love commune where I stayed for several months. I wanted to be part of what seemed to be so exciting but don't think I really enjoyed it. How my mum coped with me then I'll never know, looking back I feel so sorry for her.'

LIVING *in Sin*

Another development that grew out of the new culture of recreational sex was unmarried couples living together. In previous decades only a handful of bohemian intellectuals and artists had dared to challenge the sanctity of marriage by openly admitting to sharing a bed without being married. To do so signified loose morals and was an affront to public decency. From the late sixties onwards the more daring couples shacked up together. Although this might lead to them getting married, more often it did not and few people justified what they were doing as a trial marriage. They were having a good time. This was easy for those who had left home to go to university but could become more complicated when parents discovered what their children were up to. 'My parents decided to come and visit me at the campus on the spur of the moment to bring me a birthday present,' says Eve Coleman. 'When they knocked at the door and came in they found me and my boyfriend in bed. It was clear from all his things in the room that we were living together. My father nearly died on the spot. He was very Victorian and I'd been keeping it from him. Mum and Dad left very quickly and I think that changed our relationship for ever. I don't think they ever really trusted me again.'

It remained difficult to live with a lover if there was no excuse to leave home – going to university, for example, or having a job in another area. Most young people stayed at home until they married and, outside the big trendsetting cities like London, it was still difficult to break the rules. Parents would not allow them to and landlords and landladies had yet

> "
> WHEN THEY KNOCKED AT THE DOOR AND CAME IN THEY FOUND ME AND MY BOYFRIEND IN BED. IT WAS CLEAR FROM ALL HIS THINGS IN THE ROOM THAT WE WERE LIVING TOGETHER. MY FATHER NEARLY DIED ON THE SPOT. HE WAS VERY VICTORIAN AND I'D BEEN KEEPING IT FROM HIM. MUM AND DAD LEFT VERY QUICKLY AND I THINK THAT CHANGED OUR RELATIONSHIP FOR EVER. I DON'T THINK THEY EVER REALLY TRUSTED ME AGAIN.
> "

183

to come to terms with the sexual revolution. 'Living together in Oswaldtwistle in 1968 was not done,' remembers Dorothy Robson, who grew up in the small Lancashire mill town. 'It was known then as "living in sin" and nobody would have given you a flat. Your parents would have disowned you and it would have been a scandal amongst the neighbours. If you wanted to live together you had to get married and that's what I did at the age of eighteen.' It was as a result of pressures like these that the average age of marriage fell to twenty-one – the lowest it had ever been – in the sixties. Young people would have to wait until the 1970s and 1980s for living together to become a rite of passage into adulthood. When it did, the average age of marriage rose sharply.

Nevertheless, all over Britain there were many young women who were willing to have a casual sexual relationship or a one-night stand. Most men couldn't believe their luck. The Pill had taken away a woman's best excuse to say no and for some it was predatory heaven. 'I had an E-Type Jag and I used to park it outside the nightclubs and you'd get birds standing by it admiring it, wanting to go for a ride,' says Alfred Roper from Derbyshire. 'Very often I'd take one off for a spin down the motorway, it were nothing to go 120 miles an hour. It were a lot easier with them being on the Pill. It was all lust. You couldn't do it in the car, I'd take a blanket and nip into a wood or behind a hedge. Or I might take them out for a meal and then bed them. I wasn't a good lover though. Once I'd had sex that were it. After that I'd drop her because I'd had what I wanted. It was a case of hop on and hop off. It were better with them being on the Pill because you didn't have to worry about using a condom or them getting pregnant. You just got stuck in and enjoyed yourself.'

ARE *you* EXPERIENCED?

But more sensitive and inexperienced young men, many of whom had been brought up to expect girls to be demure and resist their advances, could find the new attitudes to sex intimidating. Now some of the most confident women were even making the first move and initiating sex. Coming to terms with this was difficult for Ian Williams, a young folk-singer drawn to Swinging London from Ireland in the late sixties. 'At nineteen years of age

I left Ireland one weekend, I didn't even tell my parents I was leaving to go to the big city in London. I had no idea what was going to happen other than that it would be more exciting. I eventually moved to north London and it was an enormous culture shock for me because I was meeting young ladies who were so forward and controlled and strong, it wasn't like that in Ireland, there the man made all the moves. My first sexual attempt was an absolute blooming disaster. I was doing a gig in a pub in Beckenham and at the end of the evening this young lady came up to me, bought me a drink and said, "Would you like to come home with me?". I was actually in shock, this was role reversal. So anyway I said "Yes", we went back to her place, a nice little flat. She was in complete control, she was a teacher, she had her own flat and she was making all the advances. I couldn't handle it, I couldn't deal with the fact that she was making me as happy as I'd hoped I'd make her. And I lost it completely. We went to bed and I couldn't even get an erection, it was all a terrible let-down and I left feeling very shamefaced.'

WIFE *Swapping*

If the Pill promoted sex before marriage, it also made sex outside marriage much safer and more attractive for bored or unhappy husbands and wives. Fear of pregnancy as the result of an affair had always been a major disincentive for married women. Now that this danger was removed they could pursue sexual pleasure more freely. A sixties fashion that attracted much publicity towards the end of the decade was partner-swapping amongst swinging couples. Although key parties often ended, predictably, in tears and marital breakdowns, some swapping was surprisingly successful, especially where both partners were keen to experiment. 'Going on the Pill had a big effect on my sex life,' remembers Eva Moffat from Manchester. 'We went from virtually having no sex in the first years of our marriage to doing it just about every night. Then my husband said we should try out the swinging scene. This was in the mid-sixties, lots of couples were trying it around us, so we tried it too. I was nervous at first but after a bit I actually loved it. I'd only ever had sex with my husband and I think that made it all the more exciting having different partners. We did it with friends to begin with, then we started advertising. We'd have drinks, then we'd pair off into different rooms. Strangely enough we weren't at all jealous, and we had even better sex together afterwards as a result of it. I know once I was sitting naked in a chair and I had five men around me who all wanted me. And none of them was my husband. It was wonderful.' Mike McGregor from Suffolk was another sixties swinger. 'I was a very successful young businessman at the time and it was thought to be a very mature and sophisticated thing to do. My wife and I were introduced to swinging in France to begin with, it was part of the jet-setting scene. It was all terribly civilized and if the woman you were with didn't fancy sex with you, or you with them, you would just talk together. It didn't worry me at all that my wife was having sex with another man. I really don't think I was jealous and she wasn't jealous of me. We split up years later but it was nothing to do with wife-swapping.'

Not So HAPPY FAMILIES

However, from the mid-sixties onwards marriages began to break down at an unprecedented rate. By 1969, the number of divorces had risen to 51,000 a year – double the total ten years earlier. It wasn't just the Pill. Women were enjoying greater freedom and independence than ever before, and those who were married were going back to work where there were opportunities to meet men other than their husbands. Sexual expectations were high. Pat Mancini was a young mother of two in Manchester in the mid-sixties. 'When you get married and have babies the sex isn't as exciting any more, well it wasn't for me. I didn't get much pleasure out of it because the love wasn't as strong, we were arguing all the time, and the marriage was going wrong. Then I got a job in a nightclub and I met Rudi, he was the organist there and we fell in love. We began an affair and all the excitement came back. It was like forbidden fruit is always sweeter. And we used to go to hotels and make love. Then we went to Blackpool together for a night and we never came back, we eloped.'

The more independent young married woman was now less likely to submit to her husband's insistence on regular conjugal rights, as Cassie McConachy from north London remembers. 'To begin with when we were married the sex was great, but it all changed when the baby was born. I was tired and I didn't want to do it so much. When you've just dealt with a bucket

full of nappies you don't feel sexy. We used to have fights. He'd say, "You're frigid" and I'd say, "Thank God". He'd say, "It's my right," but to me he didn't have a right, it was my body. I've always said that's the one thing I came into the world owning and I wasn't going to be told otherwise by him. I was very independent and I wasn't going to be told what to do. And that was probably one big reason why the marriage ended.'

Many of the trends that began in the sexual revolution of the late sixties would grow and come to fruition in the 1970s and later. The women's movement, in part a reaction to sexual exploitation by predatory men, was only just beginning in Britain in the sixties. So, too, was the gay liberation movement, given confidence and some legal protection in its struggle for rights by the legalization of homosexuality in 1967. But much had changed between 1950 and 1969. In the early fifties the majority of women were virgins when they married. By the late sixties virgin brides were in a minority. The institution of marriage had taken a battering which, for better or for worse, it would never recover from; and this lifelong monogamous partnership was now only one option amongst many. There had been a big increase in the sexual expectations of both men and women, many of whom were not willing to put up with the sexual privations of the past. Sexual choice exercised by the individual, both inside and outside of marriage, had become part of the modern lifestyle.

Family life was less of an attraction for many women in the sixties.

1950

Labour wins general election; Clement Attlee is prime minister
Petrol rationing ends after ten years
Legal aid comes into force in Britain
Eagle and *Dan Dare* comics launched
The Peak District is designated Britain's first national park
J. Sainsbury opens its first self-service store in Croydon
The first episode of *The Archers* goes on air

1951

The Festival of Britain celebrates the country's post-war recovery; visited by 8.5 million people
Spies Guy Burgess and Donald Maclean flee to the Soviet Union
Iron and steel industry nationalized
Conservative government elected; Winston Churchill is prime minister
12 million gallons of petrol blaze at Avonmouth dock, Bristol in UK's biggest peacetime fire
Miss Sweden wins first Miss World contest in London

1952

Last great London smog kills 4000
George VI dies on 6 February
Identity cards abolished
Britain tests its first atomic bomb
Tea comes off rationing
Last tram is seen on the streets of London
Jet age starts with first scheduled Comet flight between London and Johannesburg
Contraceptive pill first manufactured
Harrow train disaster leaves 112 dead
New Musical Express publishes Britain's first pop music chart

1953

Coronation of Elizabeth II
Edmund Hillary and Sherpa Tenzing conquer Everest
Iron and steel industry denationalized
Korean war ends
England wins the Ashes

1954

Mass vaccination of children against polio
Bill Haley's 'Rock Around the Clock' released
H-bomb tested at Bikini atoll
Roger Bannister runs the four-minute mile
End of food rationing
Opening of Kidbrooke, the first purpose-built comprehensive school

1955

Anthony Eden replaces Churchill as prime minister; Conservatives win general election
Commercial television begins with launch of ITV
Ruth Ellis is the last woman to suffer the death penalty in Britain
London declared a smokeless zone
Blue jeans sweep Britain
New Highway Code published
Donald Campbell breaks the water-speed record in *Bluebird*

1956

Clean Air Act attempts to end the smogs
Premium bonds go on sale.
First nuclear power station comissioned at Calder Hall in Cumbria
Suez crisis
Rock Around the Clock causes riots in cinemas

1957

Prime Minister Harold Macmillan declares, 'Most of our people have never had it so good'
Russia launches *Sputnik 1*; start of space race
Two commuter trains collide in fog at Lewisham killing 92
British H-bomb tested at Christmas Island
European Economic Community formed
Bill Haley and the Comets tour Britain

1958

Eight miles of the M6, first stretch of motorway, opens in Lancashire.
Yellow lines and parking meters appear on streets.
Campaign for Nuclear Disarmament founded; first march from Aldermaston
Notting Hill race riots
Members of Manchester United football team die in a plane crash
Coal rationing ends
Thalidomide drug causes birth defects
Debutantes presented at court for the last time

1959

Harold Macmillan re-elected with slogan 'You've never had it so good'
First section of M1 motorway opened
Britain suffers worst fog for seven years; chaos on roads
Hovercraft makes maiden cross-channel voyage
Launch of the Mini Minor
First postcodes used to sort mail
Cod war with Iceland
Buddy Holly, the Big Bopper and Richie Valence die in plane crash
Duty-free alcohol available at airports

1960

National Service ends
First NHS hearing aids issued
Princess Margaret marries 'commoner' Antony Armstrong-Jones
New pound note goes into circulation
Penguin Books' first run of *Lady Chatterley's Lover* (200,000 copies) sells out on day of publication; trial for obscenity begins in October
Europe's first 'moving pavement' opens at Bank tube station

1961

Contraceptive pill, Conovid, goes on sale
Russia puts first man in space: 27-year-old Yuri Gagarin
The Beatles make their debut at the Cavern Club, Liverpool
Betting shops legalized
MOTs introduced by Ministry of Transport
Millionth Morris Minor rolls off production line
Immigration controls announced; entry to be curbed by voucher system

1962

Cuban missile crisis
Astronaut John Glenn becomes first American to orbit earth
Smallpox outbreak
Beatles rejected by Decca record company
London's last trolleybuses retire
Telstar satellite launched; live TV signals sent across the Atlantic

1963

John F. Kennedy assassinated
Harold Macmillan resigns as prime minister; Sir Alec Douglas-Home succeeds him

BBC withdraws ban on mentioning sex, religion, politics and royalty in comedy shows
Beatlemania grips Britain
Great Train Robbery

1964

Labour government elected after 13 years of Conservative rule; Harold Wilson is prime minister
Mods and rockers clash on Clacton beach
Government announces mass closure of railways
BBC2 goes on air with *Play School*
Mary Quant knocks Paris fashion as 'out of date'
Miniskirt arrives

1965

Winston Churchill dies
Post office tower, highest building in Britain (620 feet) opens
Television ban on cigarette advertising
Rent Act reintroduces rent control
Abolition of death penalty
First Race Relations Act
Trial of Myra Hindley and Ian Brady for Moors murders; both sentenced to life imprisonment
Mary Whitehouse sets up the National Viewers and Listeners Association

1966

England wins the World Cup
Aberfan avalanche disaster in Wales kills 144, including 116 children
John Lennon says Beatles 'are more popular than Jesus Christ right now'
Barclays Bank introduces the Barclaycard, the first credit card
Labour wins general election with an increased majority

1967

North Sea oil pumped ashore at Easington, Co. Durham
Abortion is legalized
Launch of Radio 1
Private homosexuality between consenting males over twenty-one legalized
Britain's first satellite, Ariel III, goes into orbit
Chancellor James Callaghan devalues pound by 14 per cent
Outbreak of foot and mouth disease

1968

Martin Luther King assassinated in Memphis, Tennessee
Family Reform Bill reduces age of adulthood from twenty-one to eighteen
Dry-cleaners charge by inch for miniskirts
Enoch Powell's 'rivers of blood' speech
Collapse of Ronan Point tower block prompts re-evaluation of high-rise housing policy
Start of two-tier postal service; stamps cost 5d and 4d
Anti-Vietnam demonstration in London

1969

Neil Armstrong, commander of *Apollo 11*, is first man to set foot on moon
Voting age lowered from twenty-one to eighteen
Concorde makes its maiden flight
Divorce law liberalized: 'irretrievable breakdown' in a marriage allowed as grounds for divorce
Maiden voyage of QE2
At Ford car plant, Dagenham, 1600 female employees win equal pay with male colleagues

INDEX

Page numbers in *italics* refer to the illustrations